TRANSPORT AND COMMUNICATIONS BULLETIN FOR ASIA AND THE PACIFIC

No. 77
Container Transportation by Railways

T0292908

United Nations

New York, 2008   ECONOMIC AND SOCIAL COMMISSION FOR ASIA AND THE PACIFIC

Transport and Communications Bulletin for Asia and the Pacific

No. 77
Container Transportation by Railways

United Nations publication
Sales No. E.08.II.F.10
Copyright © United Nations 2008
All rights reserved
Manufactured in Thailand
ISBN: 978-92-1-120540-4
ISSN: 0252-4392
ST/ESCAP/SER.E/77

ESCAP WORKS TOWARDS REDUCING POVERTY AND MANAGING GLOBALIZATION

Editorial statement

The *Transport and Communications Bulletin for Asia and the Pacific* is a peer-reviewed journal published once a year by the Transport and Tourism Division (TTD) of the United Nations Economic and Social Commission for Asia and the Pacific (ESCAP). The main objectives of the *Bulletin* are to provide a medium for the sharing of knowledge, experience, ideas, policy options and information on the development of transport infrastructure and services in the Asian and Pacific region; to stimulate policy-oriented research; and to increase awareness of transport policy issues and responses. It is hoped that the *Bulletin* will help to widen and deepen debate on issues of interest and concern in the transport sector.

Traditionally, most Asian countries have relied on maritime transport for their export and import trade. However, the continuing evolution of containerization along with the successful implementation of various land transport infrastructure development projects at the subregional and regional levels, including the ESCAP initiated Asian Highway and Trans-Asian Railway networks, have created new opportunities for extending the opportunities of globalization to inland locations in both landlocked and transit countries.

With these developments, railway container traffic has shown the ability to meet shippers' requirements for efficient international services. For example, between 2001 and 2005, the numbers of twenty-foot equivalent units (TEUs) carried along the Trans-Siberian Railway increased by over 200 per cent. Other notable achievements include 250 per cent growth in the number of TEUs on the Malaysia-Thailand landbridge since its first year of service in 1999 and 83 per cent growth in international TEUs on Indian Railways in fiscal year 2004/2005 over 2000/2001. New international container block-train services have also been launched. In March 2002, the railways of Belarus, Mongolia and the Russian Federation launched an international container block-train service between Brest and Ulaanbaatar, followed two months later by a similar initiative by the railways of China and Mongolia with the launch of a regular service between Tianjin and Ulaanbaatar. These services proved popular with shippers and became the precursor of the extended service launched in March 2005 between Hohhot in China's Inner Mongolia Autonomous Region and Duisburg in Germany. In 2005, cross-border rail traffic between India and Pakistan (Munabao-Khokropar) was also reopened.

Similar interesting developments in container transportation by railway have taken place between the west and the east coasts of the United States of America. The present arrangement allows containers from Asia unloaded from vessels on the west coast to be delivered on the east coast in 72 hours, which is reportedly four to six days faster and less costly than the all-water route.

The above-mentioned examples show there is growing acceptance that railways have an important role to play in the national and international movement of goods. There are a number of factors that speak in favour of greater utilization of rail transport in Asia, and between Asia and Europe, including: (a) the long land transport distances within and across Asia and between Asia and Europe; (b) the sustainability of the rail mode in terms of its reduced impact on the environment and its greater energy efficiency; and (c) the ability of rail to clear landside port areas quickly to avoid congestion.

In recognition of these advantages of rail transport and growing demand for freight movement, many Governments have taken initiatives to promote container transportation by railway. These include planning and implementation of new intermodal facilities, inter-country cooperation and private sector participation. Interventions by the public and private sectors have resulted in positive results both at the national and regional levels and ushered a new era of regional cooperation in trade and transport development in the region. Experiences, ideas, and information about these developments need to be shared for their wider consideration for possible replication and implementation by decision makers and policy planners. Against this background, *Container transportation by railways* was chosen as the theme for the current issue of the Bulletin. Six articles are included in the volume.

The United Nations Economic and Social Commission for Asia and the Pacific launched the Asian Land Transport Infrastructure Development (ALTID) project in 1992. The long-term objective of the project was to assist member countries in planning and developing transport infrastructure able to serve the unprecedented surge in international trade between Asian countries and their main trading partners outside the region. The ALTID project was articulated around three components, namely: the Trans-Asian Railway (TAR), the Asian Highway (AH) and facilitation of land transport. The first article reviews the progress made in developing the TAR since the inception of the ALTID project and assesses the challenges and opportunities for a greater utilization of railways across the Asian region. The article also reviews international cooperation in promoting transport development in the region.

The rapid economic growth of the Indian economy in recent years has created huge demand for transportation services. Indian Railways (IR) has registered significant growth in freight and passenger transportation. To meet the growing demand for such services, IR has launched many important initiatives to increase its capacity and improve the quality of service. Notable among these initiatives include development of dedicated freight corridors, running of double and triple stack container trains, introduction of modern rolling stock, technological upgrading, and involvement of the private sector. The second article reviews these recent developments in India. It also presents an interesting case study on a public-private partnership project to develop a 270-km new railway line to connect a port with the main railway network of IR.

The third article also relates to Indian Railways. While the second article discusses the whole range of initiatives in the railway sector, the focus of the third article is on the development of container freight operations by a government-owned company. Indian Railways started container transportation in the mid-1960s with the use of a special type of small containers for the carriage of domestic freight. The Container Corporation of India Ltd. (CONCOR), a wholly-owned government company took over IR's infrastructure of inland container depots (ICDs) and started providing services to shippers at dry ports for warehousing, customs clearance, consolidation, disaggregation and other terminal facilities as well as feeder road services. CONCOR soon diversified into handling and carriage of intra-country freight in ISO containers. The third article describes the success of CONCOR in intermodal transport development in India as well as its success as a "blue chip" company.

The focus of the fourth article is on recent development in container transportation by rail in the Russian Federation. Structural reforms have been undertaken by the Russian Railways (RZD) to create a competitive business environment in container transportation that can capitalize on the natural advantages of railways. RZD established in 2006 a subsidiary for this purpose called TransContainer as a joint-stock company. The article provides an account of development in container transportation by TransContainer and the progress that has been made so far.

The Ministry of Transport in Thailand will take the lead role in implementing the strategic agenda of the Government in Transport and Logistics Network Optimization. The target of this agenda is to establish an integrated transport network and logistics management system which will cover the activities of collection and distribution of goods and transhipment, both at national and regional levels. Within the strategic agenda, there is a clear policy statement specifying that the Government will be responsible for rail infrastructure investment while the role of the State Railway of Thailand (SRT), a public enterprise under the Ministry of Transport, will be restricted to network management and administration and carriage of passengers. In the future, SRT would compete with private sector operators who will be allowed to invest in their own locomotives and rolling stock for providing carriage of goods services.

The fifth article discusses the on-going and planned future developments of the railway sector in Thailand.

The landbridge is an interesting concept in intermodal transport development that was first conceived in the early 1960s to promote a more efficient means of shipping between East Asia and Europe. The landbridge service involves a combination of land and sea transport as an alternative to transportation service entirely by sea. Many landbridge services are now operated in the world. One of these services in Asia and the Pacific is the landbridge container train operation between Malaysia and Thailand jointly operated by the railways of the two countries. The sixth and last article describes different aspects of this landbridge service.

The *Bulletin* welcomes analytical articles on topics that are currently at the forefront of transport infrastructure development and services in the region and on policy analysis and best practices. Articles should be based on original research and should have analytical depth. Empirically-based articles should emphasize policy implications emerging from the analysis. Book reviews are also welcome. See the inside back cover for guidelines on contributing articles.

Manuscripts should be addressed to:

The Editor
Transport and Communications Bulletin for Asia and the Pacific
Transport and Tourism Division, ESCAP
United Nations Building
Rajadamnern Nok Avenue
Bangkok 10200, Thailand

Fax: (662) 288 1000, (662) 280 6042, (662) 288 3050
E-mail: escap-ttd@un.org; quium.unescap@un.org

TRANSPORT AND COMMUNICATIONS BULLETIN FOR ASIA AND THE PACIFIC NO. 77

CONTENTS

Page

Editorial statement iii

Pierre Chartier   The Trans-Asian Railway 1

Mohammad Jamshed   Container transportation by railways
in India: Challenges and initiatives 25

Raghu Dayal   CONCOR in the vanguard of India's
intermodal development 47

Petr Baskakov   Container transportation by rail in
the Russian Federation 75

Chula Sukmanop   Container transportation by rail:
Which direction will Thailand pursue? .. 83

A. Valautham   The development of container
landbridge train services between
Malaysia and Thailand 99

ACRONYMS

AH	Asian Highway
ALTID	Asian Land Transport Infrastructure Development
ASEAN	The Association of Southeast Asian Nations
BIMSTEC	Bengal Initiative for Multi-Sectoral Technical and Economic Cooperation
CFS	Container Freight Station
CONCOR	Container Corporation of India Limited
DFC	Dedicated Freight Corridor
ECE	Economic Commission for Europe
ECO	Economic Cooperation Organization
ESCAP	Economic and Social Commission for Asia and the Pacific
FCL	Full Container Load
FEU	Forty-feet Equivalent Unit
GPPL	Gujarat Pipavav Port Limited
ICD	Inland Container Depot
IR	Indian Railways
IRU	International Road Transport Union
KTMB	Malaysian Railway
LCL	Less than Container Load
OSJD	Organization for Cooperation of Railways
PRCL	Pipavav Railway Corporation Limited
RZD	The Russian Railways
SAARC	South Asian Association for Regional Cooperation
SRT	State Railway of Thailand
TAR	Trans-Asian Railway
TEU	Twenty-feet Equivalent Unit
UIC	International Union of Railways

THE TRANS-ASIAN RAILWAY

Pierre Chartier*

ABSTRACT

For a number of years Asian economies have been attracting attention for their dynamic growth with most countries enjoying GDP growth rates and employment levels that surpass those of their main trading partners in Europe and North America.

The result is an impressive increase in international trade among Asian countries as well as between Asia and the rest of the world as evidenced by the increase in TEU throughputs in all of Asia's main international maritime ports.

The need to carry these trade volumes between ports and production or consuming centres keeps the development of efficient land infrastructure high on the agenda of transport policymakers. It also gives rail transport an opportunity to play a critical role in the emergence of modern logistics in Asian countries.

The activities of ESCAP in relation to the development of the Trans-Asian Railway network have for many years serve as a catalyst for policymakers to benchmark trends, define a common vision, adopt joint programme of actions and create a new partnership for regional economic integration.

BACKGROUND

At its 48th session[1] in April 1992 the United Nations Economic and Social Commission for Asia and the Pacific (ESCAP) launched the Asian Land Transport Infrastructure Development (ALTID) project. The long-term objective of the project was to assist member countries in planning and developing

---

*   Economic Affairs Officer, Transport and Tourism Division, United Nations Economic and Social Commission for Asia and the Pacific (ESCAP).

[1]   The Commission holds an annual session at which high-level government officials of ESCAP member countries review and adopt its programme of work. It is the main legislative organ of ESCAP.

a transport infrastructure able to serve the unprecedented surge in international trade between Asian countries and their main trading partners – primarily in the European Union and North America – and amongst Asian countries themselves. Although not limited to containerized traffic, the surge in international trade materialised most visibly in the ever growing number of containers passing through Asia's ports. But while these volumes showed the dynamism of Asian economies, they also highlighted a need for most countries to upgrade their transport infrastructure. Indeed, the existing road and rail networks were often ill-prepared to accommodate the sudden influx of goods and transport planners were put to the task of urgently revising their countries' transport master plans to enhance national capacity while, at the same time, giving greater attention to international connections.

As the new trade patterns arising from globalization were making requirement for cross-border linkages more pressing, countries of the Asia-Pacific region turned to ESCAP as a natural forum to harmonize and coordinate a number of policies and actions. The present paper reviews the distance travelled since the inception of the ALTID project and assesses the challenges and opportunities for a greater utilization of rail across the region.

I. THE LEGISLATIVE MANDATE OF ALTID

From its very start the ALTID project was articulated around three components, namely: the Trans-Asian Railway (TAR), Asian Highway (AH) and facilitation of land transport, with the objective of improving intraregional and interregional transport links as part of the ESCAP secretariat's efforts to assist member countries in addressing the challenges of globalization by providing countries with a tool to access the world's markets. This commitment had – and to this day still keep – a particular resonance for landlocked countries. The specific activities being undertaken under the ALTID project are defined, monitored and – if need be – reoriented by the ESCAP regional member countries at the annual Commission. They are then incorporated in specific work programmes which are implemented in close collaboration with the member countries as well as a number of other international and/or subregional organizations.

In addition to the Commission, senior officials of member countries assess and define the activities of ESCAP at specific sector-oriented events. In this regard, the work in the area of transport has received enhanced scrutiny and high-level endorsement at a series of ministerial conferences organized at five-year intervals.

The Ministerial Conference on Infrastructure held in New Delhi in October 1996 launched the New Delhi Action Plan that defined a set of activities to be implemented at the regional level and seeking to focus policy attention on promoting more efficient infrastructure and services taking into account economic, social and environmental considerations. Phase I activities (1997-2001) assisted member countries in enhancing their national capabilities and improving transport efficiency with significant progress made towards the formulation of intra- and interregional linkages through the Trans-Asian Railway, the Asian Highway, facilitation and shipping-related programmes.

A second Ministerial Conference on Infrastructure held in Seoul, Republic of Korea, in November 2001 adopted the Seoul Declaration on Infrastructure Development in Asia and the Pacific and mandated activities to be undertaken during Phase II (2002-2006) of the New Delhi Action Plan, thereby recognizing the vital role of ESCAP in assisting its member countries in dealing with transport-related issues in a coherent manner at the regional and subregional levels. The Declaration gave ESCAP a renewed mandate to continue to pursue the development of the Trans-Asian Railway and Asian Highway networks with particular focus on formalizing the two networks and coordinating future work towards the identification of an integrated intermodal transport system, including linkages to and from the main ports and container terminals in the region.

Finally, a third Ministerial Conference on Transport held in Busan, Republic of Korea, in November 2006, adopted a Regional Action Programme (RAP) for Transport Development in Asia and the Pacific. The RAP recognizes the Asian Highway and Trans-Asian Railway networks, formalized through related intergovernmental agreements, as two major building blocks for the realization of a vision of an international integrated intermodal transport and logistics system for the region. The activities to be carried under Phase I (2007-2011) of the RAP aims inter alia to promote an integrated approach to transport planning with a view to facilitating the emergence of efficient logistic in the region. An important aspect of these activities is the development of efficient connection to hinterland areas to move away from the past pattern of development which has seen economic benefits concentrating mostly in coastal areas.

II. THE IMPLEMENTATION OF ALTID

In turning intentions into reality several considerations dictated a pragmatic approach. One consideration was the sheer scope of the project itself in terms of the geographical area, i.e. nearly the entire Asian continent, which it encompassed.   Another one was the disparities in land transport network development in the countries and subregions concerned, and, finally, the resource availability of individual member countries.   As a result, a specific strategy was adopted for the implementation of ALTID.   This strategy comprised the four following elements:

1.   Major emphasis on project implementation at the subregional level.   This was particularly important to make the project more manageable by ESCAP, while reinforcing the ownership of the member countries through the full involvement of existing subregional groupings as partners in the implementation process.   Such major regional groupings were, for example, the Association of South-East Asian Nations (ASEAN), the Economic Cooperation Organization (ECO), the South Asian Association for Regional Cooperation (SAARC) and later the Bay of Bengal Initiative for Multi-Sectoral Technical and Economic Cooperation (BIMSTEC).

2.   A step-by-step approach through a series of corridor studies to assist in the formulation of rail and road networks, the establishment of minimum route standards and requirements as well as the identification of physical and institutional bottlenecks impeding transport efficiency and, consequently, constricting the trade capabilities of countries.

To assist member governments in identifying the respective networks, a set of criteria was adopted (see Box 1) with emphasis on minimizing the number of routes to be included in the networks and making maximum use of existing infrastructure.

Box 1. Criteria for including specific links into TAR and AH networks

- Capital-to-capital links
- Connections to main industrial and agricultural centres
- Connections to major sea and river ports
- Connections to major container terminals and depots

3.   Focus on the facilitation of land transport at border crossings through the promotion of relevant international conventions and agreements as an important basis for the development of trade and tourism. The tool for doing so was ESCAP resolution 48/11 of 23 April 1992 on Road and rail transport modes in relation to facilitation measures through which the

Commission recognized that harmonized transport facilitation measures at the national and international levels were a prerequisite for enhancing international trade. Resolution 48/11 lists seven international conventions (see Box 2) which ESCAP promotes at the regional and subregional levels with a view to assisting member countries access global markets by improving the efficiency of transport and reducing the associated costs.

Box 2. International conventions listed in ESCAP Resolution 48/11

- Convention on Road Traffic (1968)

- Convention on Road Signs and Signals (1968)

- Customs Convention on the International Transport of Goods under Cover of TIR Carnets (1975)

- Customs Convention on the Temporary Importation of Commercial Road Vehicles (1956)

- Customs Convention on Containers (1972)

- International Convention on the Harmonization of Frontier Controls of Goods (1982)

- Convention on the Contract for the International Carriage of Goods by Road (1956)

---

4. Finally, in implementing the ALTID project, promotion of close *international cooperation* with other United Nations agencies, including ECE and UNCTAD,[2] as well as other governmental and non-governmental organizations such as the International Union of Railways (UIC) and the Organization for Cooperation of Railways (OSJD), the International Road Transport Union (IRU) and International Road Federation (IRF) has been an important aspect of the strategy adopted by ESCAP. Through the development of synergies between programmes, the efforts of each organization or agencies remained more focused and the limited resources available were optimized. Most importantly, through this process of partnership, the ALTID project gained widespread international recognition and received greater focus by national governments in the definition of policies. For example, through an ECE/ESCAP joint programme of work, the two regional commissions are developing activities to implement ESCAP resolution 52/9 of 24 April 1996 on Intra-Asia

---

[2]   ECE – Economic Commission for Europe. UNCTAD – United Nations Conference on Trade and Development.

and Asia-Europe land bridges. The joint programme gives new momentum to the formalization and operationalization of the Trans-Asian Railway and Asian Highway networks with focus on specific issues such as building the missing links and giving specific importance to the development of those land transport linkages that provide access to and from major ports for the landlocked countries of Asia. This issue was highlighted in Resolution 54/199 adopted in January 2000 by the United Nations General Assembly which recognized that the higher cost of transport for landlocked countries is an obstacle to their economic development compared with other countries and that their limited access to sea ports restrict their ability to compete effectively on the international market. Recognizing the need for the international community to increase its focus on related issues, the international ministerial conference on transit transport cooperation was held in Almaty in August 2003, and a comprehensive Programme of Actions was defined aiming to secure access to and from the sea, improve the competitiveness of exports, reduce the costs of imports, address problems of security and operational efficiency along trade routes.

III. THE TRANS-ASIAN RAILWAY COMPONENT OF ALTID

The Trans-Asian Railway (TAR) project was initiated in the early 1960s with, at the time, the objective of providing a continuous 14,000-km rail link between Singapore and Istanbul (Turkey), and possible onward connections to Africa and Europe. This link therefore offered the potential to greatly shorten distances and reduce transit times between countries and regions, while being a catalyst for the notion of international transport as a tool for trade expansion, economic growth and cultural exchanges.

The international events that punctuated the 1960s, 1970s and early 1980s influenced the momentum of the concept during these three decades. However, with the political and economic changes that took place in the region in the 1980s and early 1990s, TAR-related activities were reactivated under the ALTID project. In 1996, the first of four major corridors studies (see box 3) reflecting the regional approach adopted to implement the project was published. The studies followed similar methodology and principles, namely: to (i) identify the links according to the ALTID criteria (see box 1 above), (ii) assess their conformity with a set of technical requirements (e.g. loading gauges, axle-load, speed), and (iii) appraise the compatibility of operational practices on both sides of different national borders to evaluate the possibility of cross-border movements (e.g. couplers, length of trains). In addition, the "software" aspects of transport were reviewed with particular attention to tariff-related issues and

Box 3. TAR-related corridor studies carried out by ESCAP

1. Feasibility study on connecting the rail networks of China, Kazakhstan, Mongolia, the Korean Peninsula and the Russian Federation (1996) – *Northern Corridor*

2. Development of the Trans-Asian Railway in the Indo-China and ASEAN subregion (1996); (countries concerned: Cambodia, China, Indonesia, the Lao People's Democratic Republic, Malaysia, Singapore, Thailand and Viet Nam)

3. Development of the Trans-Asian Railway: Trans-Asian Railway in the Southern Corridor of Asia-Europe Routes (1999); (countries concerned: Bangladesh, China, India, Islamic Republic of Iran, Myanmar, Pakistan, Sri Lanka, Thailand and Turkey)

4. Development of the Trans-Asian Railway: Trans-Asian Railway in the North-South Corridor Northern Europe to the Persian Gulf (2001); (countries concerned: Armenia, Azerbaijan, Finland, Islamic Republic of Iran, Kazakhstan, Russian Federation and Turkmenistan)

the institutional framework pertaining to the passage of goods across borders. Finally, two crucial infrastructure-related elements were also considered, namely: (i) the existence of break-of-gauge points along specific linkages with an assessment of possible solutions to overcome this apparent technical incompatibility, and (ii) the existence of so-called 'missing links' making end-to-end movements impossible on some of the linkages.

The ***break-of-gauge*** issue. The mainline railway networks making up the TAR network incorporate five different track gauges,[3] i.e. 1,676 mm, 1,520 mm, 1,435 mm, 1,067 mm and 1,000 mm.[4] A break-of-gauge occurs when the railways of neighbouring countries have different track gauges posing a problem of operational discontinuity.[5] The rail border crossings at which a break-of-gauge occur on the Trans-Asian Railway network are indicated in Box 4 (see also Map 1). Various techniques exist to overcome these discontinuities. They include transhipment, bogie exchange and the use of

---

[3]   The track gauge is the distance between the inner surfaces of each rail and is conventionally measured in millimetres.

[4]   It must be noted that other gauges are also found in some countries (e.g. 762 mm in India) but these line are not part of the Trans-Asian Railway network.

[5]   Discontinuity of track gauge also occurs within individual domestic railway networks. Such is the case, for example, in Bangladesh or India.

Box 4. Countries located on the TAR network between which a break-of-gauge occurs

1. China (1,435 mm) and Viet Nam (1,000 mm)

2. China (1,435 mm) and the Russian Federation (1,520 mm)

3. China (1,435 mm) and Mongolia (1,520 mm)

4. China (1,435 mm) and Kazakhstan (1,520 mm)

5. Democratic People's Republic of Korea (1,435 mm) and the Russian Federation (1,520 mm)

6. Islamic Republic of Iran (1,435 mm) and Turkmenistan (1,520 mm)

7. Islamic Republic of Iran (1,435 mm) and Azerbaijan (1,520 mm)

8. Turkey (1,435 mm) and Armenia (1,520 mm)

---

adjustable bogies.[6] While it cannot be denied track continuity between countries would be desirable, the interruption caused by break-of-gauge does not have to be a major obstacle to the commercial attractiveness of international rail services. Certainly so when it comes to international container block-train services. With limited exceptions, break-of-gauge occurs mostly at border points where a range of operations already require trains to observe mandatory stops. These operations are generated by railway needs (e.g. change of locomotives, change of crew) or the requirements of other administrations (e.g. Customs, border police, etc.). Well-designed and well-organized facilities allow for transhipment to take place within the time allocated for these other activites, the disappearance of which cannot yet be realistically envisaged. In the least optimized case of a train hauling 45 container flats carrying two 20-ft containers each and on the basis of 4 minutes per move with only one crane in action, total transhipment time would take 6 hours. This duration represents a fraction of total end-to-end transit time over landbridge distances of several thousands kilometres.

The *'missing link'* issue. A 'missing link' is the absence of physical linkages between the railway networks of neighbouring countries or an absence of continuous railway infrastructure within one country, often due, in this latter case, to local geography. Missing links between networks of neighbouring countries are due either because the link was never there in the first place, or

---

[6] Adopting measures to gradually standardize gauges or resorting to dual gauge operation are also possible options, albeit more readily applicable when the break-of-gauge occurs within individual domestic railway networks.

Map 1. Trans-Asian Railway Network

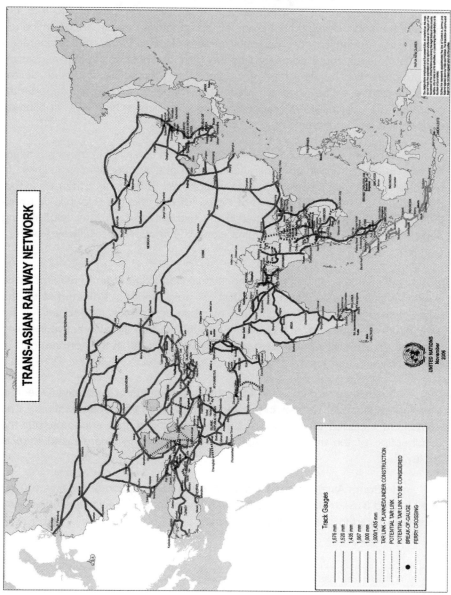

because it ceased to exist due to political events. Bridging the former[7] will require a joint approach by the railways concerned and by their respective governments. Such elements as the importance of the link in regional economic development or trade and how a particular project fits into the national transport development plans of the countries concerned will influence the decision to consent to a particular project. However, the traffic-generating potential of each route compared to the cost of constructing the necessary infrastructure will no doubt be a crucial factor, especially if private sector investments are to be sought. Meanwhile, bridging and, more importantly, operating the politically-induced missing links, requires a high-level of bilateral cooperation and understanding.

In recent years tangible progress has been achieved in moving forward towards the construction and operationalization of a number of missing links. In North-east Asia rail infrastructure was established to reconnect the railways of the Democratic People's Republic of Korea (DPRK) and the Republic of Korea (ROK). Trial runs took place between the two countries in May 2007 raising hope of future full operation of trains along the Trans-Asian Railway Northern Corridor.

Work is also under way in the Islamic Republic of Iran to reconnect the country's rail infrastructure with that of neighbouring Pakistan with the completion of work and inauguration of cross-border services scheduled for early 2008. The railways of the Islamic Republic of Iran are also active in laying tracks to connect their rail system with that of Azerbaijan in the northern part of the country.

Meanwhile, in February 2007, the governments of Azerbaijan, Georgia and Turkey signed a framework agreement to strengthen cooperation. The Agreement includes the Baku-Tbilisi-Kars rail project that encompasses the construction of the missing link between Akhalkalaki in Georgia and Kars in Turkey.

In South Asia, India has sanctioned the construction of the first 100 km of a planned 315-km line to its border with Myanmar and feasibility studies have been completed for the remaining 215 km.[8]

---

[7]   It must be noted that the construction of missing links may result in additional break-of-gauge points. Such will be the case, for example, when the link between the Islamic Republic of Iran and Pakistan is completed.

[8]   "Trans-Asia gaps to be plugged", *International Railway Journal,* May 2007.

Finally, some signs of movement are also perceptible in South-east Asia where in the past ten years an ad hoc working group has worked under the aegis of the ASEAN secretariat to look at ways to concretize the Singapore-Kunming Rail Link (SKRL) project. Work has started in China's Yunnan Province on a US$ 1.9 billion 350-km line from Dali to Rueli on the Myanmar border. China is also active on other sections of the TAR network with the construction of a 142-km section from Yuxi to Mengzi to the west of the existing metre-gauge line to Viet Nam and a 559-km line from Yuxi to Mohan to connect with the Lao People's Democratic Republic. Chinese railway corporations have also submitted to the Government of Viet Nam a feasibility study for the construction of a US$ 438 million 128-km line from Ho Chi Minh City to the Cambodian border provided it is matched by a line to Phnom Penh on the Cambodian side of the border.[9] Meanwhile, under technical assistance from Thailand work is under way to build a 3.5-km line section to extend rail infrastructure across the friendship bridge from Nongkhai (Thailand) to Thannaleng (the Lao People's Democratic Republic) as a first step towards a full connection to Vientiane, and the Government of Malaysia has donated to Cambodia the track components necessary to the reconstruction of the 48-km missing link between Poipet and Sisophon. Once in place, the section will allow cross-border rail movements between Cambodia and Thailand.

Over fifteen years into ALTID, the TAR network looks as shown in Map 1 with each corridor presenting different characteristics in their configuration and operational readiness. In the Northern Corridor,[10] there is a high level of operational readiness. In the Southern Corridor, a number of missing links hamper the development of international traffic and the priorities given to their developments vary between countries. In the Indochina and ASEAN subregion, the need to develop subregional rail linkages is now receiving full acceptance and related activities are being implemented by the ASEAN secretariat under the above-mentioned SKRL project, although funding is so far a stumbling block. In the North-South Corridor linking Northern Europe to the Persian Gulf, activities are being undertaken by the countries concerned to promote traffic along the corridor in an effort to capitalize on shorter transit times by rail as compared to maritime shipping.

---

[9]   "China backs Cambodian link", *Railway Gazette International,* July 2007.

[10]   Please refer to Box 3 for countries concerned by each corridor.

IV. TRANS-ASIAN RAILWAY, TOMORROW: OPPORTUNITIES AND CHALLENGES

A. The Intergovernmental Agreement

There is a growing acceptance that rail has an important role to play in the national and international movements of goods and people. A number of features speak in favour of a greater utilization of rail transport in Asia. (i) Twelve of the 30 landlocked countries of the world are located on the Asian continent with the nearest ports often several thousands of kilometres away, (ii) the distances linking the main origin and destination, both domestically and internationally, are of a scale on which railways find their full economic justification, (iii) the reliance on ports to connect national economies to the world's markets with the need to clear landside port areas quickly to avoid congestion, especially in the context of growing containerization and the development of intermodal transport, (iv) a number of countries are major exporters of mineral resources in the logistic of which rail transport plays a crucial role, (v) the continuing surge in the volumes of goods being exchanged, and (vi) the recognition of rail as an environmentally friendly and safe mode of transport.

Recognizing the above and also realizing that future growth in demand could no longer be met by an expansion in road infrastructure, governments of the region negotiated and adopted the Intergovernmental Agreement on the Trans-Asian Railway Network. Of the 28 member countries directly concerned by the Agreement, 18 signed the Agreement at the Ministerial Conference on Transport held in the Republic of Korea in November 2006, while the Government of India signed the Agreement at United Nations Headquarters in New York in June 2007. The current status of signatories is summed up in Box 5. The Agreement was developed with the idea that it will play a catalytic role in the coordinated development of railway infrastructure in Asia. The Working Group planned under the terms of the Agreement will meet every two years and will be a forum within which transport policymakers and railway managers will define a common vision, adopt joint programmes of actions, identify investment requirements and sources, and benchmark progress. It was also thought as a tool to evaluate investment requirements along international corridors and strengthen the case for railway expansion in loan negotiations with financial institutions such as the Asian Development Bank, the Islamic Development Bank or the World Bank. The first meeting of the Working Group will be organized as soon as the Agreement enters into force. Entry into force

---

Box 5. Intergovernmental Agreement on the Trans-Asian Railway Network – Status of signatories

Potential signatories:

Afghanistan, Armenia, Azerbaijan, Bangladesh, Cambodia, China, Democratic People's Republic of Korea, Georgia, India, Indonesia, Islamic Republic of Iran, Kazakhstan, Kyrgyzstan, the Lao People's Democratic Republic, Malaysia, Mongolia, Myanmar, Pakistan, Republic of Korea, Russian Federation, Singapore, Sri Lanka, Tajikistan, Thailand, Turkey, Turkmenistan, Uzbekistan and Viet Nam

The 19 signatories as of 31 July 2007:

Armenia, Azerbaijan, Cambodia, China, India, Indonesia, Islamic Republic of Iran, Kazakhstan, the Lao People's Democratic Republic, Mongolia, Nepal, Republic of Korea, Russian Federation, Sri Lanka, Tajikistan, Thailand, Turkey, Uzbekistan and Viet Nam

The Agreement remains open for signature at United Nations Headquarters in New York until 31 December 2008.

---

will occur on the ninetieth day following the date on which the governments of at least eight member States have consented to be bound by the Agreement.

To date the Trans-Asian Railway Network comprises of 81,000 km of lines of international importance identified through the corridor studies mentioned in the earlier part of this paper. Completing the network as shown on Map 1 requires building nearly 6,500 km of missing links for an estimated investment of US$ 15 billion. Promoting the construction of these missing links and promoting their operationalization will certainly be high on the agenda of the Working Group as they may have deep repercussions on the patterns of transportation within Asia as well as between Asia and Europe.

For example, when the reconnection of the railways of the Islamic Republic of Iran and Pakistan is supplemented by the construction of the link between the Islamic Republic of Iran and Azerbaijan, through-movements of cargo will become possible between Moscow and New Delhi over a rail distance that is substantially shorter than its maritime equivalent, i.e. 7,800 km for rail vs 14,000 km for shipping. Meanwhile, exploiting the reconnection of railways across the Korean Peninsula through the restoration of regular operation between the Democratic People's Republic of Korea and the Republic of Korea would boost economic exchanges in the Peninsula itself and through-land transport from the port city of Busan to Europe will become possible along what will be the longest transcontinental landbridge in the world (over 12,000 km). Furthermore, with the prospect of connections with the railways of China and the Russian Federation becoming a reality, the outlook of transportation in North-East Asia will be transformed. In much the same way, the future connection between the railways of Cambodia and Thailand as well as the extension of the Thai rail infrastructure into the Lao People's Democratic Republic will allow an extension of the container landbridge that was successfully co-launched in 1999 by the Malaysian Railway (KTMB) and the State Railway of Thailand (SRT). Through the new infrastructure and the existing landbridge services Cambodia and the Lao People's Democratic Republic will both gain access to Malaysia's main ports, a most important benefit for the Lao People's Democratic Republic in view of the country's landlocked characteristic.

But putting the missing links in place will not in itself guarantee a transfer of traffic from road and shipping to rail. Two characteristics of railway that will bear heavily on the future development of freight by rail along the TAR network will be the structure of rail operation on the different railway organizations transited by the TAR routes, the ability of rail to attract investment from both public and private sectors and the commercial skills of railway organizations in determining services and pricing them.

B. Attracting investment

The traditional source of finance for infrastructure development in countries of Asia have been allocations from government budgets with the role and significance of these sources varying from country to country, reflecting such elements as the stage in social, economic and political development, the levels of disposable income, and the extent and efficiency of taxation regimes. Direct observation of the gap between required and existing transport facilities and services calls for massive investments to: (i) maintain existing railway assets, and (ii) expand these assets. Given the long lead time associated with rail infrastructure projects and their usually low return on investment, it is doubtful that they will ever be attractive to the private sector. In this context, rail infrastructure should typically continue to be a national asset provided by governments under its ownership and management. Governments could optimize the cost of providing the infrastructure through a system of usage charges that each individual government could fix at different level depending on practices vis-à-vis other modes and the necessity to ensure a level playing field for all modes. This would most likely be welcome by both rail users and rail operators as a means of safeguarding the high level of safety that rail transport is credited for while creating the opportunity for market sensitive pricing.   An added benefit is that by keeping ownership of transport infrastructure in general as well as responsibility for its long-term planning, governments will be able to exercise leverage to guarantee intermodal integration so that each mode can be used to deliver the best it has to offer.

Initiatives by governments to develop rail infrastructure along the Trans-Asian Railway should also recognize that the emergence of a truly operational network able to meet the current and future transport requirements of a globalized economy calls for greater balance between projects deemed of international importance and those of a purely national nature. This balance is all the more difficult to strike in a context of limited budgetary resources.

Aware of this problem, the ESCAP secretariat has initiated a study aiming to generate among its member countries a common global vision of rail infrastructure development. The process of multilateral consultation that the study will launch will help member governments agree on priority projects, make efforts at achieving greater synchronization in their implementation and acquire greater leverage to approach international financial institutions for assistance.

While government financing will be crucial for further rail infrastructure development, it does not mean that state authorities will not fund future projects in partnership with the private sector. Despite high growth in all areas of business activities, RZD's Vice-president acknowledged in late 2006 that a shortage of investment funds was leading to reduced throughput because of infrastructure problems on around 8 per cent of RZD's total track length and further recognized that the company had already gained very positive experience with public-private partnerships on a variety of projects to build new lines and upgrade the existing ones.[11]

Outside the provision of rail infrastructure a number of areas linked to rail operation lend themselves well to the involvement of private sector such as, for example, rolling stock procurement, yard operation, service definition/ marketing, property/land usage development. In rolling stock alone pressure is building up on most railways of the region to renew and expand their aging fleets of locomotives, coaches and wagons to cope with existing traffic and meet new demand. Requirements are high on all railways. The President of RZD recently stated that updating rolling stock was one of his company's priorities but recognized that the US$ 6.6 billion earmarked for the purpose

---

[11]   "RZD faces a bright future", *International Railway Journal*, October 2006.

over the period 2007-2010 was not sufficient for timely modernization and for handling the traffic volumes envisaged in RZD's long-term plan for 2010-2015.[12] He illustrated his point by estimating that to meet the target for 2010 RZD needed to buy at least 20,000 new vehicles a year. He indicated that establishing and partly floating a new freight operating company could generate the finances for the required wagons.

In this respect examples abound in many countries – both in and outside the ESCAP region – of industries financing and operating their own rolling stock. This is particularly the case for heavy traffic such as coal, petroleum products or grain moving in unit trains between production sites and processing plants. For a number of years RZD has allowed independent private companies to own and use their own rolling stock, including locomotives. In India, Container Corporation of India (CONCOR) which was corporatized in 1988 and commenced business in 1989 with the aim of developing multimodal logistics using IR's network as the backbone for their operations also owns an increasing share of its fleet of specialized container platforms. The company recently acquired high-speed container flats capable of speed of 100 km/hour 1,900 such wagons have already been deployed on the main container routes.[13] The practice may be worth receiving attention from cash-strapped railways in need of rolling stock renewal. In South-east Asia, the container landbridge operation established by Malaysian Railways (KTMB) and SRT between Port Klang (Malaysia) and Bang Sue (Thailand) quickly turned into a success story with container volumes soaring from 21,640 TEU in 2000 to 58,224 TEU in 2004, i.e. 170 per cent over the period. However, 2006 traffic levels were back down to 42,520 TEU. The reason was a high rate of online failures of trains due mostly to locomotive breakdowns. Twenty-nine per cent of trains entering Thailand experienced online failures in 2005, 33.7 per cent in 2006 and in the period January to May 2007 the figure had risen further to 37.5 per cent.[14]

The system of letting private operators own and use rolling stock offers a number of advantage for railway organizations. Not only does it free investment capabilities for infrastructure projects, but it also leaves the responsibility and cost of matching rolling stock and demand in both volumes and nature with the private operators thereby exploiting their ability to react quicker to market-demand.

---

[12]   "Investment will underpin RZD reforms", *Railway Gazette International,* January 2007.

[13]   Website of Container Corporation of India at www.concorindia.com. See more on CONCOR in a companion article in this volume.

[14]   Source: State Railway of Thailand.

C. Developing commercial skills

A few years ago the debate about the future of railway primarily focused on privatization. May be by lack of sufficient successful experiences to base a credible case on, talks now tend to give greater emphasis on public-private partnerships and commercialization of railways. Commercialization rests on a concept and a principle. The concept is that given the proper incentive and scope to exercise their managerial talent, there is no obvious reason why railway managers could not drive their organizations towards the same benefits that private managers are often credited with. Meanwhile, the principle is that railways do need to provide services which are demand-driven, customer-oriented, and results-led. In other words, if the market (or government in case of subsidized passenger services) will not pay for a service, it will not be offered. In this respect, if governments request that unprofitable services be maintained, they should be prepared to cover the difference between revenues and costs. While the President of RZD indicated that cross-subsidization of passenger services should be terminated, he also indicated that this should not be at the expense of passengers and the head of the Federal Passenger Agency created under RZD's reform package further stressed that the low level of competitiveness and profitability from passenger operation did not result from poor management but from the conditions imposed by the state to provide rail services for social reasons.[15]

If the above infers that capital will not be attracted to an unprofitable and over-regulated sector, it also means that when working in an unregulated sector subject to the rules of competition, flair and judgment have to be exercised to the definition, pricing and marketing of services. When this is the case, railways can prosper as is illustrated by the case of the KTMB-SRT landbridge (see above) until the service started to be plagued by locomotive failures. The success story of CONCOR provides another vivid illustration of railway managers' ability to serve a market. Over the decade 1997-2006, volumes transported by CONCOR soared from 703,542 TEU to 1,930,562 TEU. At the other end of the ladder, the 30 per cent rate increase imposed in early 2006 by RZD on Trans-Siberian services sent shippers from the Republic of Korea en masse into the arms of ocean carriers. As a result, total transit cargo railed to the Finnish border through the port of Vostochny in the Russian Far East – i.e. the mainstay of RZD's intermodal traffic along the Trans-Siberian main line – dropped by 90 per cent. The extent to which the 30-35 per cent reduction agreed in early 2007 by Russian Tariff Authority to raise the competitiveness of Trans-Siberian services will attract lost traffic back onto rail

---

[15]   "Russian rail revolution enters final phase", *International Railway Journal,* October 2006.

will depend largely on how Korean shippers have been locked into their deep sea contracts with ocean carriers.[16]

These three cases illustrate that commercial success is in sight when services are developed keeping in mind a set of basic elements such as the cost of providing a particular service, shippers' needs, the assessment of the value of the service provided in a shipper's distribution system, and the offer made available by competing modes. This means that some market segments may not be so rewarding and may be left out, while others should be investigated without being overcharged. This is particularly important if railways are to capitalize on their intermodal quality to develop traffic and generate much needed resources to finance development along the routes of the TAR network.

V. MOVING PEOPLE OR CARRYING FREIGHT: WHAT MISSION FOR THE TRANS-ASIAN RAILWAY NETWORK?

The ALTID project was launched with the objective of addressing the mobility requirements of both people and goods. Today this objective remains unchanged. However, in practical terms, operationalizing the TAR network calls for a more discerning approach. While individual sections of the network – and mostly over their domestic stretch – will continue to cater for passenger traffic, the corridors in the network have been identified with international trade in mind and will primarily serve freight. This choice is also dictated by the need for railways to generate revenues of their own at a time when national budgets have to address a host of issues (e.g. health, education or national defence) that cannot be covered by the working of market forces. As seen above freight can generate substantial earnings, while passenger services are usually maintained at a heavy cost to governments. In addition, the TAR network has been designed with long-distance carriage in mind. Once affluent enough to travel long distances, people will most likely prefer air travel over surface transport, with due provisions being made for the special cases of future services aimed at exploiting the real – but nonetheless narrow – niche of railway tourism. Currently cross-border passenger traffic remains limited and takes place mostly between countries of Central Asia, the Caucasus region, and the Russian Federation in line with travel habits inherited from the Soviet Union.

So if freight, what kind of freight? As previously mentioned a number of ESCAP member countries are major exporters of mineral resources in the

---

[16]   "Trans-Siberian seeing thaw", *Containerisation International*, March 2007.

logistic of which rail transport plays a crucial role. This intrinsic advantage of rail in the movement of heavy bulk is clearly illustrated by traffic along the recently-inaugurated line section between Mashhad and Bafq in the Islamic Republic of Iran. Since its opening in May 2005 the line, which provides the landlocked countries of Central Asia with access to the Port of Bandar Abbas on the Persian Gulf, has handled considerable quantities of bulk liquids. Compressed gases, aggregates, chemical products and steel coils are also moving over the line with much of the traffic to and from countries of Central Asia.[17] Heavy hauls of coal, oil or petroleum products are also a common feature of rail operation in China and the Russian Federation.

The above shows that when it comes to serving freight, the TAR network is a versatile network. However, the concept of an Asia-wide railway finds its full justification in exploiting the intermodal nature of international trade. It is estimated that container traffic accounts for more than 50 per cent of international trade in volumes and about 90 per cent in value. Global container market reached 115 million TEU in 2006 and is growing at 10 per cent per year.[18] With 20 of the world's 30 top container ports located in the ESCAP region, countries are only too well aware of the phenomenon and the pressure it puts on their ports as well as land transport infrastructure.

American intermodal traffic by rail provides an interesting basis for comparison. In many instances, railroads have signed contracts with Trans-Pacific shipping lines with services adhering to schedules of shipping lines. These tailored services have obviously played a major role in the growth of intermodal traffic between 1984 and 2002 during which weekly services departing from the west coast have increased from 1 to 241 to move 60 per cent of containers arriving by sea for destinations inland. Overall, traffic tripled during the period 1980 to 2002 with intermodal accounting for 20 per cent of railroads' revenues in 2002.

Of course, there is a huge difference between Asia's government-owned, mixed-traffic railways and the North American privately-owned, heavy-haul freight railways. However, at least two key features of American railroads are not without relevance for the region, namely: the alliances they have developed with shipping lines and their integration into the global logistics chains of manufacturers.

---

[17]   "Transit freight booms on Bafgh – Mashhad link", *Railway Gazette International,* January 2007.

[18]   " 'Tsunami of containers' offers opportunities and challenges for freight operators", *Railway Gazette International,* May 2007.

This last point is indeed essential if railways of the region are to prosper and attract private sector investment in a number of areas, especially rolling stock and intermodal facilities. Forecast shows that the expected increase in container movements worldwide will be larger for intra-Asian trade than for other directions of trade. Moreover, a study recently conducted by Japan's Ministry of Economy, Trade and Industry indicated that 70 per cent of intra-Asian trade is intermediate goods used in production with half being driven by final demand outside Asia.[19] Turning this potential into a source of substantial earnings requires that rail moves from a uni-modal approach to service-definition and operation to become a functional element of dynamic logistics chains that extend beyond – and are often controlled outside – national borders. For example, in 2006, Chinese ports alone handled about 30.9 per cent of the TEU handled in the world's top 30 container ports.[20] Yet, only an estimated 1 per cent of the containers loaded and discharged at the country's ports used rail for their overland travel despite the long distances involved. Inland costs to the coast from the provinces are often more expensive than the shipping cost from the port in China to the destination port.[21] Similar situations are also found in other countries of the region such as India where land freight cost is more than double in countries with more developed transport/logistics, i.e. US$ 0.07 per ton-km vs US$ 0.02 in Canada or US$ 0.037 in Japan.[22]

Developing rail traffic through improved logistics is an area of future cooperation between governments and private sector. The container landbridge between Malaysia and Thailand is an early precursor of such partnership. Trains have direct access from KTMB's main track to the Northport terminal to enable straddle-carriers to load and unload containers, thus saving time for customers. Currently, there are three major landbridge block-train operators – T.S. Transrail, Freight Management and Infinity Logistics Sdn Bhd – that operate on specific window-time on KTMB tracks. The operators offer a total of 16 block-train services to and from various international inland container depots in Thailand and Northport.

Private-sector rail operation is also off the starting-block in India. 14 private operators have been granted licences to operate container services on IR's network. In July 2007, APL India Lynx (APLIL) started operation between Loni ICD near Delhi and Jawaharlal Nehru Port in Mumbai. APLIL is

---

[19]   "Japan looks for improved competitiveness in Asia", *Containerisation International*, August 2007.

[20]   "Top slots", *Containerisation International*, March 2007.

[21]   "China's logistics solutions", *Containerisation International*, August 2007.

[22]   ESCAP draft study report *Promoting the role of the Asian Highway and Trans-Asian Railway Networks: intermodal interfaces as focus for development*, August 2007.

a joint venture between Hindustan Infrastructure Projects and Engineering (HIPE) and the Singapore-based shipping line Neptune Orient Line which is a parent company of American President Line (APL). The service was well-received by shippers with over 1,000 TEU carried in its first month of operation. APLIL now plans to invest US$ 60 million over the next two years to buy new equipment and start services on other corridors. The company also has plans to develop its own ICD in the northern state of Haryana.[23]

Intermodal traffic along the Trans-Siberian line in the Russian Federation is also expected to expand with Russian Railways implementing projects aiming to boost corridor capacity to 1 million TEUs per year. Traffic along the corridor had grown at a steady pace until the sudden rate increase imposed by Russian Railways in early 2006 (see above). European Rail Shuttle, a company based in the Netherlands, recently completed a trial run of fifty-two 40-ft containers of computer parts from Shenzhen in China to a destination in the Czech Republic offering a door-to-door transit time of 17 days, i.e. half the travel time offered by maritime shipping.[24]

In addition to the above and apart from the line construction projects already mentioned in the course of this paper, watchful eyes should also be kept on efforts to develop container terminals as well as ventures onto new territory such as the development of double stack container services. Chinese Railways, to name but one, have started to develop a network of 18 major intermodal rail hubs and 40 mid-size stations strategically located at ports and inland economic centres as part of the US$ 240 billion plan by the Ministry of Railways of China to upgrade and expand its network to 100,000 km by 2020. Each facility will cover 6 to 12 sq km and have a capacity to handle 200,000 – 300,000 containers a year with double-stack container services eventually linking these hubs.[25] In this latter area, India already stepped ahead of other railways when IR inaugurated its first double-stack container service in March 2006 between the Kanakpura ICD near Jaipur and Pipavat port in Gujarat.[26] Trials are also taking place on RZD's network with surveys of loading gauge clearance completed on routes from Moscow to Nakhodka, Novosibirsk, Murmansk and the Finnish border.[27]

---

[23]   "APL India Lynx invests more, adding another train to JNP/Lori service", *Containerisation International,* August 2007.

[24]   "European Rail Shuttle joins Trans-Siberian Rail club, after successful trial", *Containerisation International,* August 2007.

[25]   "The Yangtze River transport Corridor", *Deloitte & Touche,* July 2006.

[26]   "IR tries double-stack service", *Railway Gazette International,* May 2006.

[27]   In *Railway Gazette International,* March 2006.

CONCLUSION

Until only a few years ago many observers were writing out rail as ever being able to regain any significance in modern-day transportation market. Fortunately, this thinking seems to have been reversed and in many countries the level of investment channelled into railways – although well below what is consented to road transport – is getting ever higher. In the ESCAP region, while the lion's share of investment in rail projects goes to China, India and the Russian Federation, railway managers in other countries are also in an upbeat mood. Rail development is very much at the core of the modern transport system that the Government of the Islamic Republic of Iran is putting in place with investments in new lines, higher axle-load, state-of-the-art signalling and telecommunication technology, and modern motive power. Since 1994 – when the Iranian government decided to increase rail's share of the transport infrastructure budget to 30 per cent – Iran has built more new railway lines than any country except China.[28] Things are also astir in South-east Asia with Malaysia and Viet Nam taking a lead in railway development. In 2006, the Government of Malaysia unveiled its 9th Malaysia Plan setting out a detailed framework for economic development over 2006-2010. Under the plan KTMB was allocated US$ 1.08 billion for infrastructure and rolling stock investment. Meanwhile, Vietnam Railways (VR) is embarking on the construction of rail connections to seaports, mines, industrial parks and key economic zones around the country. VR expects to spend US$ 912.5 million on construction alone during 2007-2010 under a mixture of domestic and foreign investments.[29] Finally, Central Asian countries are also in an investment mood with, for example, Kazakhstan seeking bids for US$ 458 million worth of projects.[30]

Under its Trans-Asian Railway activities the ESCAP secretariat has identified a number of international rail corridors. Surveys among governments of the region have indicated that these activities have already provided substantial assistance to member countries by outlining guidelines on route alignments, technical standards and operational as well as commercial requirements for the development of railway lines and roads of international importance. The identified TAR network (and its road equivalent) is increasingly being included in national and subregional programmes for transport development. This is a first step. A second step is now to ensure that the

---

[28] "Iran plans 50 per cent network expansion as Mashhad-Bafq line opens", *Railway Gazette International*, May 2005.

[29] "Vietnam Rail Corp Plans Modernisation", *Asia Pulse*, 22 May 2007.

[30] *International Railway Journal*, July 2007.

sections of each corridor are effectively developed according to commonly-agreed standards. Indeed, the attraction of container traffic to the TAR network depends in large measure on rail being able to offer cost effective and reliable services as compared to its competitors in the various corridors making up the network. In this regard, it is imperative that operational impediments be removed. While, as mentioned above, different track gauges do not have to be a major obstacle, incompatible train length and load, different axle-loads, incompatibility in rolling stock design (i.e. couplers, braking systems), different route capacity and train operation practices on individual rail systems along a specific corridor constitute much bigger barriers to efficiency and may create anxiety among shippers. In this area, it is hoped that the Working Group on the TAR network that will be established once the Intergovernmental Agreement enters into force will address these issues in a bold and forward-looking manner. It is also hoped that the Working Group will yield a common vision on priority investments and lead to a better synchronization between national procedures when it comes to taking projects off the drawing board and into implementation.

Step 3 is about operating the network. Once the technical bottlenecks have been removed, attention should focus on institutional bottlenecks and the joint definition and operationalization of services. In the longer term, corridor-based organizations with the authority to act on behalf of their constitutive railway administrations in areas such as service-definition, tariff-setting and marketing as well as the possibility of bulk-selling trainload-based capacity to private sector need to be considered. The development of joint border stations to implement a "one-stop-shop" concept under which all rail and non-rail operations by the relevant administrations of two neighbouring countries are performed at one single location would also be a step towards greater operational efficiency. Synergies between rail and road as well as the development of cross-over points with maritime, inland water and air transport are only starting to be explored and require more in-depth work. All these activities would certainly gain from an infusion of private sector.

The rapid economic development of the ESCAP region presents a range of complex issues for the transport systems of member countries. Making rail a prime choice for shippers dictate a tall agenda such as providing capacity, procuring rolling stock, ensuring interconnectivity between modes, putting in place the necessary regulatory framework to invite private sector, and – last but not least – developing human resources in adequate numbers and with the needed technological skills. These issues constitute a daunting task for many countries in terms of planning and resource-mobilization. It also is a task that requires an increasingly high level of international cooperation as the requirements for cross-border movements parallel the growth in international trade. But daunting as they are, these issues constitute a fascinating blue-print of actions for railway managers of the future. They also provide an area for ESCAP to facilitate dialogue and identify and promote best practices for the greater benefits of its member countries.

Box 6. Useful ESCAP website

Further information on related ESCAP activities can be obtained through ESCAP's Transport and Tourism Division website.

- **www.unescap.org/ttdw/index.asp**

- **www.unescap.org/ttdw/index.asp?MenuName=AsianHighway**

- **www.unescap.org/ttdw/common/TIS/TAR/tar_home.asp**

Finally, increasing the efficiency of inland transport is not a matter of transport planning only. The economic and social implications are enormous. Studies have shown that level of income, trade growth and income growth decline as distances from coastal areas increase. The results are: (i) social inequalities between cities within a certain perimeter of ports and the more remote provincial areas, and (ii) population shifts to cities that are not always prepared to receive a sudden influx of migrants. A recent study found out that China spends about 18.5 per cent of its GDP on logistics costs, compared with 10 per cent in the United States of America and Europe.[31] With a GDP of US$ 1,932 billion, the savings would finance more than half what the country plans to invest to realize its 2020 rail vision.

When environmental concerns are thrown on top, the increasing relevance of the rail mode and the impact of rail services beyond the mere transport sector of countries become even more apparent. These considerations were very much in the minds of ministers and transport policymakers who gathered for the Ministerial Conference on Transport in the Republic of Korea in November 2006. In the declaration that concluded the Conference, they clearly expressed a common desire to make the Trans-Asian Railway Network a major building block in the definition of an international integrated intermodal transport and logistics system serving the future economic prosperity of Asia and the well-being of its citizens.

---

[31]   "China's logistics solutions", *Containerisation International,* August 2007.

CONTAINER TRANSPORTATION BY RAILWAYS IN INDIA: CHALLENGES AND INITIATIVES

Mohammad Jamshed*

ABSTRACT

The Indian economy is growing at an unprecedented rate. The multi-sectoral growth has posed humongous challenges to the infrastructure sectors, especially transportation. Indian Railways has registered significant growth in both freight and passenger transportation during last three years. Seized of the challenges from different sectors including transportation of containers by railways, Indian Railways has launched some important initiatives including construction of Dedicated Freight Corridors, Public-Private Partnerships in rail infrastructure development, induction of modern rolling stock, technological upgradation, and new experiments for running double stack container trains in electrified sections and triple stack container trains on diesel routes. Due to these initiatives, the years ahead are likely to witness tremendous growth in container transportation by railways in India enabling and sustaining an efficient logistics chain and the much needed support to the growth of international trade.

INTRODUCTION

Many interesting and intriguing shifts in national development policies and priorities are taking place to face the challenges of globalization. National economies are gearing up to face some of the most dramatic changes in the core sectors specifically manufacturing, services and infrastructure. Challenges posed by inter-dependability of countries and a sense of their coherent co-existence largely as a result of economic integration have resulted in some of the most talked about developments in many parts of the world.

*   Senior Vice President (Marketing and Operations), Pipavav Railway Corporation Limited, 1st Floor, Jeevan Tara Building (Gate-4) No. 5, Parliament Street, New Delhi – 110 001. The views expressed by the author are his own and do not necessarily reflect the views of the Government of India.

South Asia too has not only witnessed these changes but emerged as one of the fastest growing regions in terms of the GDP growth. The Indian and Chinese economies are in the lead globally with GDP growth rate hovering around 9 per cent per year. The proliferation of markets and relocation of manufacturing activities have also brought significant shifts in regional and international trade to and from the countries in the Asia-Pacific region. The multi-sectoral growth has necessitated development of infrastructure including power, transport, and communication. Transport has now become the core of infrastructure in national priorities in many countries such as India. Huge public sector investments along with public-private partnership arrangements are being planned for strengthening, upgradation and expansion of transport networks. The international trade and to a large extent the domestic trade consider intermodal transportation to be the most suitable and convenient means of ensuring seamless logistics chain.

Containerization of cargo and its transportation by railways is a late development in South Asia compared to container transportation by surface transport in the United States of America and Europe. The growing international and intraregional trade has reinforced the thinking that efficient intermodal transportation of containers is an inescapable requirement to reduce unit cost and transit time. The development of container transportation by railways in India is an interesting story. Great strides have been made in this sector during the last five years. Major challenges have been identified and addressed to by taking major initiatives by the Government and lately by the private sector.

I. RECENT TREND IN TRANSPORT DEVELOPMENT

Asia-Pacific region

A frenzied growth in some of the Asia-Pacific economies has put additional pressure on their infrastructure sectors, the demand for which outpaces the GDP growth. The economic development as a result of centralization of manufacturing activities, services and consumption centres demands an efficient transport system both for passengers and freight. However, the share of surface transport in international trade even today hovers around 5 per cent. This has been largely on account of development of improved maritime connectivity between continents and regions providing efficient and low cost transportation solutions against inadequate and slow development of surface transport systems. In addition, countries with larger geographical spheres and long coast lines, transport sizable volume of goods to other ports in the same country by coastal shipping. The development of surface transport has, to a large extent, remained restricted on account of huge costs involved in providing fixed infrastructure like construction of roads and rail infrastructure. The lack of surface transport links also affects the seamless movement of freight traffic across the regions rather adversely.

To address this problem, huge investments are being made to develop rail and road networks in the Asia-Pacific region. China and India are rehabilitating, strengthening and expanding their railway networks to cater to the huge transport demands of their economies.

Rail and road networks spanning across regions are being brought together under multilateral agreements like the Asian Highway Agreement and the Trans-Asian Railway Agreement. Globalization alongwith liberalization of national economies has also resulted in sizable increase in international trade that is largely intermodal i.e. movement of containers involving more than two modes of transport such as sea, road and rail. The container transportation by railways in the last few years has acquired new dimensions across the globe especially in the Asia-Pacific region.

Container transportation by railways

It is generally agreed that the first freight containers were used in the United States of America around 1911. However, it took another 50 years for container operations to become a major component in freight transportation. Container movement witnessed manifold increases in the last few decades. Over a period of time and with the development of ISO containers, certain amount of standardization and uniformity could be achieved globally. The container trains and ships could accommodate larger volumes of containers with ISO specifications. Intermodal operations became swift and efficient. The larger container ships with the capacity of upto 8,000 TEU started calling at growing number of ports and carried cargo for not only transhipment by feeder shipping services but also for long-haul transportation of containers by rail to their destinations in hinterlands. With the induction of latest container ships with a capacity of 14,500 TEU (Emma Maersk), the development of rail and road network alongwith longer and heavier trains have become necessary.

According to a forecast by ESCAP[1] the annual average growth rate of world's container traffic would be about 6.5 per cent during the period 2002-2015. China has acquired the leading position in the world container

---

[1]   ESCAP and AITD (2007). *Toward an Asian Integrated Transport Network* (ST/ESCAP/2399).

transport market accounting for 20 per cent of world container handling and about 50 per cent of the Asian total.

The ESCAP forecast also estimates that the port throughput of international cargo will increase from 240.5 million TEU in 2002 to 576.4 million TEU in 2015, representing about 6.9 per cent annual average rate of growth. It is also estimated that during the same period the international container port throughput in Asia and the Pacific will grow from 133 million TEU to 352 million TEU indicating an annual average growth of 7.7 per cent. This would also increase the region's share from 55 per cent to 61 per cent of the total container traffic. Container transhipment will also grow from 30 million TEU in 2002 to 76 million TEU by 2015. The estimate also indicates that about 927 new container berths would be required for the handling of the new container traffic across the world, of which 569 berths would be required in the ESCAP region alone.

The trend of growth of container traffic poses a serious challenge to national infrastructure facilities and equipment. The growth indicators have been well received in countries such as China and India and many initiatives have been launched in the infrastructure sector in the last few years. In the following sections container transportation by rail in India is discussed alongwith the current situation, the challenges posed and initiatives undertaken and planned.

II. INDIAN ECONOMY AND INDIAN RAILWAYS – AN OVERVIEW

India is one of the fastest growing economies in the Asia-Pacific region next only to China, having achieved a growth rate of over 9.2 per cent in 2006-2007. The GDP growth rate of over 9 per cent has been targeted for the XIth Five Year Plan period of 2007-2012. All the core sectors of the economy have shown significant trends of growth resulting in growing demands on the existing infrastructure. Plan outlays for the transport sector have gone up to 14.8 per cent of the total outlay during the Xth Five Year Plan period.

Recent announcements by the Government reiterate that huge investments would be required in this sector. Railways in India has also been declared as the core of infrastructure. Apart from moving a sizable volume of passenger traffic, its freight traffic largely consist of long-haul bulk commodities including coal, iron ore, cement, food grains, fertilizer, and petroleum, oil and lubricant products. The growth in these sectors of the economy directly results in growth of freight traffic on Indian Railways (IR).

IR has one of the largest rail networks in the world with 63,332 route km equivalent to 109,808 track km. It carries over 1.83 million tons of freight and 15.68 million passengers everyday.[2] It is not only the single largest employer with 1.41 million employees but its operations also account for almost 2.8 per cent of country's GDP directly. In the last few years IR has witnessed an unprecedented growths in both passenger and freight traffic. Although railway operations are undertaken on mixed use basis (passenger and freight trains share the same infrastructure), the freight tonnage which was 557.39 MT in 2003-2004 has gone up over 726 MT in 2006-2007. The freight revenue constitutes two-thirds of IR's total revenue earnings (over US$ 15 billion in 2006-2007) with passenger revenues contributing for one-third.[3] During the last three years IR has achieved a growth rate of over 8 per cent and brought down its operating ratio from 92 per cent in 2003-2004 to 78.7 per cent in 2006-2007.[4] IR essentially moves a select group of commodities on long hauls (average hauls are over 600 km). In addition to the transportation of bulk commodities, it also undertakes operation of container trains and parcels.

The railway network is spread across the length and breadth of the country connecting resource centres with consumption centres, ports with hinterlands, major cities/population centres, sub-urban areas and even inaccessible and remote areas. Over 50 per cent of its freight and passenger traffic, however, moves on six major routes which connect the four metropolitan cities of Delhi, Mumbai, Kolkata and Chennai. These routes are called the Golden Quadrilateral and its diagonals, which accounts for 25 per cent of the network. Strengthening of these vital rail routes is being accorded high priority.

IR's Five Year development plans are part of the national Five Year Plans. The XIth Five Year Plan (2007-2012) projections indicate that IR would be targeting to achieve a freight traffic of 1,100 MT and passenger traffic of 8,400 million in the year 2012. In order to achieve these targets, IR would be making an unprecedented investment of over US$ 60 billion, a sizable portion of which will be coming from internal resource generation and public-private partnership arrangements. During this period two Dedicated Freight Corridors planned at a cost of US$ 8 billion are likely to be completed, connecting Mumbai-Delhi and Kolkata-Delhi. It will also include major feeder routes connecting major production areas with consumption centres and ports with hinterlands. It has also been decided that during the XIth Five Year Plan period

---

[2]   *Indian Railways Year Book 2005-2006.* Published by the Ministry of Railways, India.

[3]   *Indian Railways Looking Ahead to Future, 2007.* Monograph, published by Ministry of Railways, India.

[4]   Operating Ratio is the ratio of working expenses to gross earnings.

the main routes of the remaining metre gauge rail sections will be converted to broad gauge in order to increase their connectivity with the main rail network and to provide seamless operations. Modernization of the rolling stock and construction of high speed passenger corridors are also planned.

Rail-port connectivity is another significant area which has been given special attention by the Government. Although all the major ports have already been provided with broad gauge rail connectivity, a few identified sections which are experiencing capacity constraints are being taken up for double tracking and gauge conversion. A number of such projects would be completed through public-private partnership arrangements. The construction of Dedicated Freight Corridors would also facilitate the movement of double stack container trains in a big way.

III. TREND IN INTEGRATED INTERMODAL TRANSPORT DEVELOPMENT IN INDIA

In the global trading system India is fast emerging as a centre for manufacturing goods and services. However, it faces tough competition from other countries in providing seamless logistics services and suffer from capacity constraints in certain sectors. Containerization of cargo and its movement across the country has significantly improved during the last decade. However, the ratio of containerized cargo to general cargo handled at ports is still about 45 per cent, which is much lower than the global figure of about 70 per cent. During 2005-2006, out of 423.4 million tons of total port cargo handled containerized cargo was about 60 million tons.[5] The trend in terms of cargo projected to be handled at the major ports indicated in the National Maritime Development Programme of the Ministry of Shipping is given in table 1.

The maritime transport is likely to play an ever growing role during the decades ahead. Indian exports crossed US$ 100 billion in 2005-2006 registering an unprecedented growth of 25 per cent. Imports have also grown significantly to US$ 140 billion. As 95 per cent of the export and import are done through the ports, this trend of growth in trade can only be sustained if the port and connecting land transport infrastructure are developed at a matching pace. Rail and road connectivity to ports is the key to seamless container operation. Currently 12 major ports in India handle 75 per cent of the total maritime cargo, which has increased from 19.38 MT in 1950-1951 to 415 MT by the end of 2006-2007.

---

[5]   National Maritime Development Programme, Department of Shipping, Government of India. Available at <http://shipping/nic.in>.

Table 1. Projections for cargo handling at major Indian ports
(in million tons)

Year	Total cargo handled	General cargo including containers		Containerized cargo	Per cent of total	Per cent of general cargo
		Million tons	Per cent of total			
2000-2001	281.10	75.05	26.70	32.22	11.50	42.90
2001-2002	287.58	83.13	28.90	37.24	12.90	44.80
2002-2003	313.53	96.43	30.80	43.67	13.90	45.30
2003-2004	344.80	105.82	30.70	51.06	14.80	48.20
2004-2005	383.77	118.65	30.90	54.76	14.30	46.20
2005-2006	423.42	130.81	30.90	61.83	14.60	47.30
2006-2007*	415.00	123.45	29.70	61.10	14.70	49.50
2013-2014*	961.55	404.15	42.00	251.40	26.10	62.20

Source: National Maritime Development Programme – Department of Shipping, Government of India – Website: http://shipping.nic.in/.

* Projected.

An integrated transport system has become the need of the time to cater to this huge demand for transportation. For this not only various modes have to be placed in position but the systems at change of transportation mode points have to be efficient. For an integrated transportation network containerization of the cargo is a basic requirement.

The growth projections for the containerized traffic in India are extremely positive indicating a huge growth rate of 15-20 per cent on an annual basis during the next 10 years. It is estimated that the Indian ports are likely to handle over 20 million TEU per year by the next 10 years from the present level of 5 million TEU. The transportation of containers to and from the ports would require efficient surface links by both rail and road. According to another estimate about 70 per cent of the containerized cargo is meant for hinterland areas which are located beyond 300 km. Out of this traffic only about 30 per cent is being currently carried by railways. The geographical spread in India with all the ports located in the south and the hinterland markets in the north necessitates that a sizable portion of this traffic is moved by the railways. Ninty per cent of the entire container handling is confined at the ports on the west coast of India with Jawaharlal Nehru Port in Mumbai handling over 50 per cent of the country's container traffic.

IV. CONTAINER OPERATIONS BY RAILWAYS IN INDIA

At present transportation of container by railway in India is being undertaken almost entirely by Container Corporation of India Limited (CONCOR), a public sector undertaking of the Ministry of Railways set up in 1989 with the prime objective of developing intermodal transport and logistics infrastructure.[6] CONCOR is engaged in the business of setting up and managing a network of rail linked and road-based Inland Container Depots (ICD) and Container Freight Stations (CFS). With its nationwide 56 container terminals and a large fleet of captive rolling stock, it has handled 2.1 million TEU during 2006-2007.

CONCOR's 41 terminals exclusively handle export-import traffic and are fully equipped with rail/road ICDs and port side container terminals. CONCOR not only provides rail services between ICDs and the ports but also between ports and hinterland. As CONCOR is primarily a rail bound service provider, its mainstay is long-haul traffic from ports to the hinterlands. It undertakes operations with a fleet of over 8,000 freight cars (flat container wagons). The normal container trains consist of 45 wagons which carry 90 TEU per train at 100 km/hour. New high speed wagons are being procured alongwith modern equipment for the ICDs. The warehouse space is being extended to 150,000 square metres with facilities for handling bonded cargo, multi-tacking, consolidation of cargo, and air cargo besides conventional transit warehouses.[7] CONCOR rates are quite competitive and in cases where these are higher than the rates by road, the coordinated transit time and the capacity to handle large volumes offset the higher charges making CONCOR a preferred service provider.

Advance information system along with cargo logistics information system has greatly helped CONCOR in managing the cargo and the terminals. Facilities for e-filing of commercial documents and container and cargo logistics system have also been made available to customers. CONCOR has achieved a cumulative annual rate of growth of over 15 per cent in the last few years. However, an analysis of the existing port traffic indicates that out of the total containerized port traffic, only 30 per cent of the total container traffic is currently being handled by CONCOR, although such traffic requires long-haul movement to the hinterland.

---

[6]   A separate article on CONCOR in this volume provides more information on its business, operational practices, performance and other matters.

[7]   www.concorindia.com – The official website of Container Corporation of India.

V. CONSTRAINTS AND CHALLENGES TO CONTAINER TRANSPORTATION BY RAIL

Capacity constrains on major rail routes

IR has achieved an unprecedented growth of 9.2 per cent in goods traffic and 7.0 per cent in passenger traffic over the last three years in sharp contrast to the usual growth rates of 3-4 per cent. This could be achieved despite capacity constraints on major routes of its network. The Golden Quadrilateral and its diagonals connecting four metro cities and some of the major ports suffer from acute capacity constraint on most of the sections. The same infrastructure carries mixed traffic i.e. freight, passenger, parcels and container trains. With passenger trains accounting for over 60 per cent of the train runs, the capacity to handle freight trains is limited. Over 50 per cent of the containerized traffic moving by rail is between Delhi and nearby destinations and Mumbai. The rail route, despite being a double line and electrified, suffers from capacity saturation on a number of sections. Apart from Mumbai and Jawaharlal Nehru port, other ports on the West coast including Kandla, Mundra and Pipavav are also connected through feeder sections with this main route. Most of these rail sections are also saturated. Capacity constraints are also significant on the rail route connecting Delhi in the north with Kolkata in the east and Chennai in the south. The projected growth of over 10 per cent in freight traffic and over 15 per cent in container traffic over the next 5-10 years is likely to put additional pressure on the existing rail routes.

Inadequate rail-port connectivity

The cargo handled at the 12 major ports has increased from 19.3 MT in 1950-1951 to 383.6 MT by the end of 2004-2005. With a future GDP growth of over 9 per cent, the development and modernization of port infrastructure would be essential to ensure global competitiveness. The capacity at various ports is likely to increase with the approved expansion programmes and introduction of modern technology. However, the capacity of the ports to handle cargo and thereby reduce the turn around time of vessels is dependent upon its capacity to evacuate the cargo quickly and efficiently. Lack of quick evacuation directly affects the turn around time of ships at major ports in India which is in the range of over 3 days at present. The estimates prepared by the Planning Commission indicate that traffic for all ports in India is likely to grow at an annual rate of 7.5 per cent. The highest rate is expected in container traffic which is likely to be over 17 per cent during the period 2003-2004 to 2013-2014. In this period, the container traffic is likely to grow from 3.90 million

TEU to 20.95 million TEU. The current share of railway in container transportation is about 30 per cent, which is likely to grow from 1.55 million TEU in 2005-2006 to over 6 million TEU by 2013-2014.

Although all the 12 major ports are connected by rail, the rail-port connectivity for some of them is inadequate. In view of the projected growth of traffic at major ports and saturated capacity of exiting routes, the single line rail sections are required to be doubled, meter gauge lines require conversion to broad gauge, and new lines are to be constructed to connect green field ports. A large number of medium and small sized ports including those in the private sector are coming up both on the East and West coasts. These ports also require efficient rail connectivity with the main IR Network for quicker evacuation of cargo.

Capacity constraints at ports

India has a long coast line extended over 7,500 km. Six major ports are located on each of the East and West coasts and handle over 75 per cent of sea borne traffic. The remaining 25 per cent is handled by non-major ports. The growth rate of over 10 per cent of port traffic over last few years demanded that the capacity at ports is expanded. The combined capacity at all the major ports was 456 million tons per annum in 2006 against the actual traffic of 423 MT in 2005-2006, indicating that there was adequate capacity to handle the present level of traffic. However, the growth projections indicate that within the next five years, this traffic is likely to go over 700 MT requiring the handling capacity at ports to be substantially increased by that time. The capacity constraints are already being experienced at not only the major ports but also at the non-major ports. The requirements include development of additional berths, deepening of channels, modernization and induction of latest cargo handling equipment and expeditious completion of port connectivity projects. Other facilities required include development of container terminals and warehouse facilities, construction of dry docks, ship repair facilities and dredging etc. The non-major ports are at different stages of development and therefore also suffer from capacity constraints.

Insufficient terminals and dry ports

Container transportation by railway is being undertaken largely to and from 56 container terminals also known as ICDs managed by CONCOR. A few container terminals are also being operated by private container operators. As the pattern of container transportation by rail is currently region specific (North India to ports), the existing terminals in North India suffer from capacity constraints. Some of the terminals which were initially located inside the cities and towns also face similar constraints in view of the severe congestion on roads for movement of trucks to and from the terminals. The infrastructure at some of the terminals is also inadequate to handle the projected growth of rail bound containerized cargo.

Technical constraints

Container operations by rail are dependent on an efficient fleet of rail freight cars and modern container handling equipment in the port sidings and also in the terminals. The present fleet of wagons for container operations is bogie low height container flat wagons. These wagons are provided with slackless draw bars, automatic twist locks and load sensing devices alongwith anti-pilferage devices and are able to run at a speed of 100 km/hour. The length of container train is limited to 45 freight cars which can carry either 90 TEU or 45 FEU. The restriction in the length of train is primarily on account of standard length of loop lines, which is 700 m in length.

The capacity of the trains to carry more containers is also restricted as container flat wagons cannot carry double stack ISO containers in the electrified sections due to the overhead electric lines. Non-availability of specially designed wagons which can carry double stack containers results in running of single stack container trains on the electrified sections. Running of double and triple stack container trains on non-electrified routes also requires removal of height restrictions due to foot over bridges, road over bridges, tunnels and railway bridges.

VI. INITIATIVES AND STRATEGIES

During the annual Budget Speech in February 2007, the Minister of Railways, India announced that container transportation by rail will be increased to 100 million tons by 2011-2012 from its current level of 20 million tons. Infrastructure would be strengthened accordingly to facilitate the movement of containerized cargo by railways. This would involve major investments in the development of container terminals, procurement of rolling stock and improvement of related rail infrastructure.[8] Some of the major initiatives launched in these regards are discussed in the following sections.

---

[8]   Minister for Railways, Government of India's Budget Speech on 26 February 2007.

Development of Dedicated Freight Corridors and throughput enhancement projects

The capacity constraints on the existing major rail routes have been identified by the Ministry of Railways and have accorded high priority in removing those constraints. Various measures for the enhancement of throughput by strengthening the existing major rail routes including upgradation of tracks, doubling of single line sections, gauge conversion, replacement of old signaling gears and electrification of sections are being initiated. The identified projects have been assigned to a separate organization called Rail Vikas Nigam Ltd. (RVNL) to ensure their faster completion. RVNL is a special purpose vehicle under the Ministry of Railways. It is currently executing 46 projects at a cost of about US$ 3 billion to expand the capacity of high density traffic routes. Fourteen of these rail projects are scheduled to be completed by 2006-2007. The construction of another 544 km broad gauge line would be completed by 2007-2008. The rest of the projects are scheduled to be completed by 2009-2010.

In addition to the above mentioned capacity enhancement works, it has been decided by IR to develop Dedicated Freight Corridors along side the major identified routes. This new concept is to ensure that the freight and passenger traffic are segregated on the busy routes and thereby create additional capacity for handling the projected growth of rail freight traffic. Two mega projects for the construction of Dedicated Freight Corridors involving construction of 2,700 route km of railway line equivalent to about 5,000 track km at an approximate cost of US$ 6 billion have been sanctioned by the Government. The western Dedicated Freight Corridor is to connect Jawaharlal Nehru Port (JNPT), Mumbai with the container terminals in Delhi area. The eastern corridor on the other hand would link the ports on the east coast of India with Delhi and Punjab. The western corridor will primarily cater to container transportation by rail. It is estimated that the Dedicated Freight Corridor will be able to handle not only the projected growth of traffic form JNPT and Mumbai ports but also other ports on the West coast which will also be connected to the corridor through feeder routes. The Dedicated Freight Corridors would be designed to run longer, heavier and double stacked container trains. It is expected that these two corridors will be completed over the next five years. In addition, IR has also decided to develop similar corridors alongside other busy routes. Feasibility studies are being conducted to assess the specific requirements and costs. It is also planned to procure new design of wagons with bigger space envelope and develop mega freight terminals/ logistics parks alongside these corridors.

Intermediate blocks and automatic signaling will also be provided along with bypasses to improve sectional capacity and faster rail movement across busy junctions. These initiatives are likely to take care of the capacity constraints being faced at present and provide additional capacity to deal with the projected growth of rail traffic specially for container transportation by railway. Various options for financing these mega projects are being explored, which include public-private partnership and assistance from multilateral and bilateral financial institutions.

Prioritization of rail-port connectivity projects

The rail-port connectivity projects have been prioritized and specifically assigned for execution by RVNL. RVNL is undertaking feasibility studies and examining the possibility of their implementation by setting up joint ventures with the private sector. Over two dozens of rail-port connectivity projects are assigned to RVNL. The Committee on Infrastructure set up by the Government, prioritized the ongoing rail-port connectivity projects for their expeditious completion. These projects include:

- Doubling of Panskura-Haldia Port railway line;

- New railway line connecting Haridaspur with Paradip Port;

- Gauge conversion of Hasan-Mangalore Port line to broad gauge;

- Gauge conversion of Palanpur-Gandhidham to broad gauge;

- Connecting Ports of Kandla and Mundra on the West coast;

- Doubling of Panvel-Jasai rail section connecting Jawaharlal Nehru Port-Mumbai;

- Doubling of Maduari-Dindigul section to facilitate movement to and from Port of Tuticorin in the south; and

- Gauge conversion of Bhildi-Samdari rail section to broad gauge for additional connectivity to Kandla Port and construction of railbridge over Mahanadi to facilitate movement to and from Paradip Port.[9]

These projects will cost about US$ 500 million. A number of these projects have already been completed. In addition, rail-port connectivity projects for Kolkata, Goa, Mumbai and Ennore ports are also being developed

---

[9]   *Road-Rail Connectivity of Major Ports,* report published by the Secretariat for the Committee on Infrastructure, Planning Commission, Government of India.

for providing new rail connectivity and strengthening of the existing rail infrastructure. With these rail-port connectivity projects completed, all the major ports would be able to handle the projected growth of traffic. Non-major ports are also being provided rail connectivity. Some of these projects are being implemented by the special purpose vehicles like Pipavav Railway Corporation Ltd. (PRCL).

The constraints restricting the port operations have also been identified and over 276 projects involving total investment of over US$ 12 billion have been proposed under the National Maritime Development Programme for implementation by 2011-2012. The Government has also permitted foreign direct investment upto 100 per cent for the construction and maintenance of ports and harbours and it is expected that an investment of about US$ 7 billion would be made by the private sector for these projects. Apart from augmenting the existing capacity at the ports, some of the larger capacity enhancement plans include an off-shore container terminal at Mumbai port, 2nd container terminal at Tuticorin port, 3rd container terminal at Mormugao port, 4th container terminal at Jawaharlal Nehru Port, multi purpose cargo berth at Kandla port and container terminal at Ennore port.

Development of terminals and logistics parks

IR also plans to develop mega freight terminals. For this, IR has collaborated with the Central Warehousing Corporation. In a recent policy announcement, IR has also asked private operators to develop ICDs and container terminals by providing the available vacant railway land. Various options for developing common user facilities are also being explored. The logistics parks and mega terminals are also planned alongside the Dedicated Freight Corridors.

Container train operations by private operators

As part of the strategy to increase the IR's share of container traffic and to introduce competition in railway container transportation, the Ministry of Railways opened up this sector to private container operators. The private container operators including logistics companies, shipping lines and transport companies may now register with the Ministry and obtain permission to undertake container operations on the IR network at par with CONCOR, which was the only entity to undertake container operations until now. Fourteen container operators have signed a model concession agreement (MCA) on 4 January 2007 with the Ministry to undertake container operations. The entry of 14 operators indicates that the scope for such ventures in view of the projected growth of container traffic and the preference of the shipping lines to move containers by railways is overwhelming. This decision of the Ministry would not only enable it to achieve the target of 100 MT of container traffic by railways by 2011-2012 but would also result in generation of additional capacity in terms of additional terminals, ICDs, logistics parks, and induction of modern rolling stock.

The private container operators under this agreement have to develop their own ICDs and procure rolling stock which would be operated by IR by levying haulage charges on container operators. This move will greatly encourage competition, improve efficiency and reduce unit cost of operation. The operators would also undertake marketing, collection and aggregation of cargo from the hinterlands to the terminals. Container operators are procuring their own rolling stock through purchase, import, lease or on rent basis. The policy is now open to other potential container operators and it is expected that many more private container operators would join the group of container train operators.

Double stack and triple stack container operations

With the unprecedented growth in India's external trade and specially that of the containerized cargo, it is expected that the number of container trains will increase manifold over the next 5-10 years. Although efforts are being made to develop Dedicated Freight Corridor and augment the capacity of existing rail network, one of the significant short-term measures to augment the capacity to handle the increased volume of traffic would be either to increase the length of container trains or to move containers in double and triple stacks. Double stack container trains also tend to reduce the unit cost of transportation and requirement of rolling stock. Taking into account the experience on the United States of America and Canada where double stack container trains are running on long hauls, incurring savings of almost 40 per cent in operating costs, IR also decided to undertake double stack container running on non-electrified sections.

A feasibility study on running of double stack container trains was undertaken by PRCL, which included detailed survey of the identified route between Gurgaon (near Delhi) to the Port of Pipavav on the West coast of India. This route was specifically selected for being non-electrified. The container trains were running on this single line route on diesel traction carrying a load of 90 TEU or 45 FEU per train in single stack. This rail route of 1,233 km from the Port of Pipavav to Gurgaon was already capacity saturated in sections causing longer transit times for trains. The only solution to increasing the throughput and quicker evacuation of the port was found to be running of double stack container trains on this route.

Detailed physical survey identified the overhead infringements by structures such as road over bridges, foot over bridges and crossing of high tension electric transmission lines etc. The survey was undertaken with the help of a special prototype structure loaded on a flat container freight car. With the help of this measuring device, all the identified locations of the infringements were physically checked. After the survey, infringements were categorized in Phase I and Phase II. Phase I indicated the infringements required to be removed for moving double stack container trains with container height of 8 ½ feet each. The Phase II infringements were those which were required to be removed for undertaking movement of double stack container trains with container height of 9 ½ feet each (High cube).

On directions from the Ministry of Railways the work on removal of infringements was taken up on a priority basis and the first double stack container train was flagged off from an ICD located near Jaipur for Port of Pipavav in March 2006. The arrangement approved for loading container in double stack was with either 2 FEU in double stack or 2 TEU in the lower section with 1 FEU on top. Initially, clearance for running of double stack container trains has been given for a speed of 75 km/hour. The double stack container trains are now successfully running between container terminals at Kanakpura near Jaipur and Port of Pipavav. It is observed that with double stack container operations, the share of container transportation by rail has increased with the same rolling stock and the overall transit time has significantly reduced.

The work of removal of infringements for enabling running of high cube ISO high containers in double stack is currently being undertaken on the Gurgaon and Port of Pipavav rail route.

Double stack container trains on electrified rail routes and triple stack on non-electrified sections

The Ministry of Railways has now decided to run double stack container trains on electrified routes and triple stack container trains with low height containers on diesel hauled route. PRCL has been asked to take up a detailed survey for this purpose. PRCL has designed low height containers matching the length and width of ISO containers but with reduced height. Taking into account the height of the container flat wagons, total height of the trains with the double stack modified container is 4,782 mm and that of triple stack container 6,691 mm. For the purpose of survey, the electrified Delhi-Pune route was selected keeping in view of the huge requirement of car transportation from the manufacturing plants in Delhi area to Southern India and movement of car from Southern Indian plants to North India. The modified containers were specially designed to carry upto four small sized cars in one container. The height of the contact wire on electrified rail routes of 5.50 m was found to be sufficient for the running of low height double stack container trains in electrified sections. However, under certain fixed structures including tunnels and bridges the height of the contact wire is lower than 5.50 m. During the survey it was also observed that it was possible to not only raise the height of the overhead wire but also lower the track at few locations to obtain the necessary clearance. At present work on providing the necessary clearance are being undertaken. It is estimated that double stack operation in electrified territories would enable movement of 360 cars per train against 120 being currently transported in modified rolling stock. Similarly triple stack container trains on diesel routes would be able to carry 540 cars in specially modified containers. Such transportation of automobiles in containers would also provide complete logistics solutions to car manufacturers. Loaded containers can be brought to the rail terminal by trucks and at the other end they can be further despatched by road to various retail outlets without involving loading and unloading at rail terminals. The project is now in the development stage.

Public-private partnership (PPP) in rail infrastructure projects

IR has a large shelf of infrastructure projects with an investment requirement of over US$ 10 billion. The public funding required to complete these projects could not be provided through the usual budgetary support. The limited funding available during the last few years resulted in thin spread of resources across many rail infrastructure projects. As a result, completion of these projects took much longer than the targeted and resulted in cost overruns. It was decided that important rail infrastructure projects which were operationally justified and financially viable, including projects for rail-port connectivity, may be taken up through public-private partnership arrangements. The PPP policy was opened to the potential beneficiaries including State Governments, port authorities and trade and industry. Participation of the Ministry of Railways in special purpose vehicle or SPVs formed under this arrangement made the scheme quite attractive. A combination of equity and debt was adopted for the financing of such infrastructure projects. The experiment has been greatly successful and a few important rail infrastructure projects have been completed in record time.

The flagship joint venture in a rail infrastructure project is Pipavav Railway Corporation Limited with an equal participation of the Ministry of Railways and Gujarat Pipavav Port Limited (GPPL), a private port company. PRCL has developed 270 km long rail connectivity to the Port of Pipavav with the Indian Railway network. Significant volumes of container and bulk cargo are being moved to and from the port.

Similar to PRCL, two other SPVs have been formed. The Hasan Mangalore Rail Development Corporation (HMRDC) and Kutch Railway Company Limited (KRCL) are two such ventures, the former connecting the port of Mangalore with Hasan, an important iron ore producing area and the latter connects Palanpur in Western India with the ports of Kandla and Mundra on the West coast. Both of these PPP arrangements involve participation of the State Government, port authorities and the private sector. All the above mentioned three rail infrastructure project companies have been able to complete the ongoing rail port connectivity projects including gauge conversion and construction of new lines in record time. Few more similar SPVs are being considered for other important rail infrastructure projects including new lines connecting ports. The PPPs in port connectivity projects have resulted in a guaranteed flow of containerized and bulk cargo on these lines and are regarded as successful ventures.

Public-private partnership project – a case study of the Pipavav Railway Corporation Limited

Gujarat Pipavav Port Limited (GPPL) a private port company was set up in 1992 to manage the Port of Pipavav. Being the first private sector port in the country located on the west coast of India in the State of Gujarat, the port did not have any rail connectivity with the IR network. The development of this private port largely depended on a broad gauge rail connectivity with the hinterland. A Memorandum of Understanding was singed between GPPL and the Ministry of Railways in 2000 for promoting a joint venture company to undertake construction, operations and maintenance of the Surendra Nagar-Pipavav Rail Project (270 km). The Government of India approved the formation of the first joint venture between the Ministry of Railways and the private sector, and the Pipavav Railway Corporation Limited was established on 30 May 2000. The PPP arrangement was to have equity contribution of 50:50 between the Ministry of Railways and GPPL. Thereafter, PRCL signed various agreements with the Ministry of Railways including Construction Agreement, Concession Agreement, Shareholders Agreement, Lease Agreement, Operations and Maintenance Agreement and Transportation and Traffic Guarantee Agreement. Apart from the equity provided by the Ministry of Railways and GPPL, debt was raised from financial institutions for undertaking construction of the project line. From the signing of the Construction Agreement in 2001, the work was completed in a record time of two years and the line was commissioned in March 2003. The commercial operation on this line started from April 2003. Since 2003-2004, the movement of cargo to and from the port of Pipavav has been steadily going up both for containers and the bulk cargo. About two-thirds of the cargo being handled on this line is by containers. In addition, other bulk commodities including fertilizer, food grain, salt, cement and coal have been transported by rail to and from the port. The traffic handled during 2006-2007 went up to 2.3 MT.

The project was awarded to PRCL by the Ministry of Railways on a 33-year concession period for operation, maintenance and undertaking of other activities. The total cost of the project was over US$ 90 million out of which US$ 50 million was provided by the Ministry of Railways and Gujarat Pipavav Port Limited on a 50:50 basis. The remaining funds were raised from the market (financial institutions/consortium of banks). The concession entitles PRCL to exercise all the rights and authorities vested in the concessionaire under the agreement. PRCL has the rights, obligations and duties of the railway administration on the project section. It has rights to commercial exploitation of the project assets and can develop, design, engineer, finance, market, procure, construct and operate the project railway, market freight services, appoint supervisors and monitor activities of contractors. It also has the rights to develop additional facilities in the project area, can quote special rates in specific cases. It receives its share of the apportioned earnings from the tariff on freight traffic originating, terminating and moving on the project railway. It also has freedom to levy and charge tariffs for container traffic on this section. Various obligations of PRCL alongwith rights and obligations of the Ministry of Railways are detailed in the Concession Agreement.

This concession was granted for a period of 33 years unless terminated earlier in accordance with the terms of the agreement. After the expiry of 33 years, the project assets will be handed over by the concessionaire to the Ministry of Railways with a provision that if the Ministry to grant a fresh concession in respect of the project railway, the concessionaire will have the first right to be awarded the new concession.

PRCL has also entered into a Traffic Guarantee Agreement with Gujarat Pipavav Port Limited and Western Railway (Zonal Railway Administration of Indian Railways). As per the Traffic Guarantee Agreement, GPPL will provide a minimum guaranteed quantity of the cargo. This was to be 1 MT during the 1st year, 2 MT in 2nd year and 3 MT from the 3rd year onwards till the termination date. Any shortfall against the guaranteed traffic will be converted into revenue and the amount will have to be paid by GPPL to PRCL. This guarantee is deemed to have been fulfilled, once the minimum guaranteed traffic has been met during the financial year.

The Traffic Guarantee Agreement ensures that the guaranteed cargo is made available by the port to PRCL and in case of non-fulfilment, a compensation is to be paid by GPPL to PRCL, which ensure its financial viability. This agreement also includes the provision that Indian Railways will guarantee sufficient rolling stock for evacuation/movement of the minimum guaranteed traffic that originates at the port. The agreement envisages that in case of non-availability of its obligations under the agreement, Western Railway is responsible for paying out compensation to GPPL. This provision ensures that the evacuation of cargo takes place from the port in time.

IR does not provide any incentives/subsidy to PRCL. However, in view of the likely traffic shortfall against the guaranteed traffic during the first four years, IR has deferred the operating and maintenance costs on a request made by PRCL for the first few years which is to be paid along with interest from 2008-2009 onwards.

The revenue sharing arrangement between the Ministry of Railways and Pipavav Railway Corporation Limited is also detailed in the O&M Agreement. The same has been further followed through a Joint Procedure Order signed between the parties wherein detailed procedure has been spelt out for the compilation of necessary data on the traffic moved over the PRCL section and for the calculation of apportioned revenue to PRCL. Bills for operations and maintenance including both the fixed costs i.e. salary and wages of employees and variable cost i.e. fuel and locomotive and wagon hire charges etc. are raised by the IR and adjustments are made out of the PRCL's share of the traffic revenue.

PRCL has obtained license from the Ministry of Railways for running its own container trains. The plan developed by PRCL involves procurement of new rolling stock i.e. freight wagons, containers and setting up of ICD/container terminals. It is expected that the investment required for the expansion of business can be raised from financial institutions and existing consortium of banks.

The management of PRCL is fully independent to manage the day-to-day work. It has to, however, supervise and monitor operations on the project line in close coordination with the local railway authorities and the Ministry of

Railways. The Board of Directors of PRCL, which is headed by the Member (Traffic), Ministry of Railways as its Chairman has equal representation from GPPL and Ministry of Railways. Major investments and policy decisions are taken by the Board of PRCL.

In addition to rail operations and marketing, PRCL also undertakes project consultancy services and transport related feasibility studies. It has conducted a number of feasibility and bankability studies for railway projects over the last three years including for construction of a new line connecting Kathmandu in Nepal with Birganj. PRCL is looking forward to entering the logistics market after acquiring its own rolling stock and setting up of CDs. It plans to provide complete logistics solutions to shipping lines and other customers both for containerized and bulk cargo. It has also taken up research and development activities for the running of double stack container trains from Jaipur to Port of Pipavav and is currently working on models and technical solution to run double stack container trains in the electrified territories and triple stack container trains in non-electrified territories.

VII. INTERNATIONAL AND REGIONAL TRADE – POTENTIAL AND POSSIBILITIES

At present, 95 per cent of India's international cargo moves by sea through the ports. The share of international cargo by surface transport including rail and road is limited to just about 5 per cent. Apart from established road connectivity between India and its neighbours including Bangladesh, Bhutan, Nepal and Pakistan, rail connectivity provides a much better transport mode for trade with the neighbours. Intraregional rail connectivity is, however, restricted by certain types of commodities, specific type of rolling stock and other trade restrictions. As is evident, broad gauge (1,676 mm) railway network is largely confined to the countries of South Asia including Bangladesh, India, Nepal and Pakistan, thereby providing potential for movement of bilateral cargo by rail without involving transhipment and change of rolling stock. India currently has two cross-border points with Pakistan i.e. one in the north (Wagha-Attari) and the other in the west (Munabao-Khokhrapar). Only one of these points i.e. Wagha-Attari is opened for both freight and passenger traffic and the other point i.e. Mumabao-Khokharapa is restricted to only passenger traffic. With Bangladesh, three broad gauge cross-border points on the western side of Bangladesh at Benapole-Petrapole, Gede-Darshana and Singhabad-Rohanpur are operational. All the three border points are exclusively for freight traffic.

Nepal is also connected by a broad gauge link with India. Regular movement of container trains takes place between Kolkata and Birganj. At present, there is no rail connectivity between India and Sri Lanka, India and Bhutan and India and Myanmar. Routes of international significance and various other intraregional corridors have been studied and identified by ESCAP and SAARC. Missing links and various other physical and non-physical barriers hindering the seamless operations have been identified on these routes. It is expected that operationalization of intraregional rail connectivity would not only provide access by the landlocked countries like Bhutan and Nepal to ports and markets but also increase the intraregional trade between the countries of the region. The potential for intermodal operations specially movement of containers by rail is immense.

CONCLUSION

India is emerging as one of the fastest growing countries in the world. It is also becoming the hub of manufacturing and services and developing as a huge consumption centre. The growth of India's international trade is now over 20 per cent annually. Despite 95 per cent of the international trade being undertaken through the sea routes, the geographical expanse of the country and the locations of its ports necessitate long-haul movement of containers from ports to the hinterlands. However, only 30 per cent of the total containers handled at the Indian ports are being transported by rail. The growth projections for the international and domestic containerized traffic and the capacity expansion plans of ports indicate that there is likely to be huge demand for transportation of containers by rail. There are constraints which presently inhibit further growth of container transport by rail. To overcome these constraints, Indian Railways has launched some major initiatives including construction of Dedicated Freight Corridors, encouraging PPPs in rail infrastructure projects, modernization of rolling stock and fixed infrastructure, development of mega logistics parks and opening of containerized transportation sector to private operators. Special efforts are also being made to introduce running of double stack container trains in the electrified territories and triple stack container trains in non-electrified sections. These initiatives are expected to significantly increase the capacity of container transportation by rail.

Rail transportation of containers in India is something worth watching during the next few years in view of the huge growth projections and IR's ambitious plans and initiatives to develop its infrastructure and take on the challenges posed.

CONCOR IN THE VANGUARD OF INDIA'S INTERMODAL DEVELOPMENT

Raghu Dayal*

ABSTRACT

Indian Railways (IR) made a rudimentary beginning with intermodal transportation of domestic shipments followed by its own 5-ton container for door-to-door transport of domestic cargo in the mid-1960s. IR also set up a nucleus of makeshift inland depots with linkages to gateways for ISO containers.

The Container Corporation of India Limited (CONCOR), a wholly-owned government company took over IR's infrastructure of inland container depots (ICDs) and provided a single-window, one-stop service to shippers at dry ports for warehousing, customs clearance, consolidation, disaggregation and other terminal facilities as well as feeder 'last mile' road services. CONCOR also diversified into handling and carriage of intra-country freight in ISO containers. A conscious thrust towards low-cost, modular construction and expansion of its network of ICDs and container freight stations, together with customer-driven business ethos has helped CONCOR win confidence of industry and business. It has also helped IR face the growing challenge from road transport for a share of the export-import traffic.

CONCOR stands today with a commendable track record and is ready to cope with emerging challenges of competition. Its management along with a compact body of professionals it has built would reckon its future as yet another opportunity to think out-of-the-box and reach new heights in intermodal transportation.

THE BEGINNINGS

Relatively a late starter in intermodal/multimodal development, India improvised some rudimentary infrastructure at some of the ports like Cochin,

*   Director (Logistics), Asian Institute of Transport Development, New Delhi, India; e-mail: aitd@vsnl.com.

Chennai (Madras), Kolkata (Calcutta) and Mumbai (Bombay) supported by makeshift rail-fed inland container depots (ICDs) at Delhi, Bangalore and Coimbatore in the mid-1980s. It was only in 1990 onwards that intermodal development came to make a significant beginning, when Container Corporation of India Ltd. (CONCOR) provided an impetus to the scheme.

While, in the 1980s, the then Ministry of Surface Transport was assigned the task of developing container infrastructure and facilities at ports, particularly at Bombay, Calcutta, Cochin and Madras, as well as the development of a new modern container port at Nhava Sheva, (called Jawaharlal Nehru Port – JNP), the Government decided to set up a separate fully government-owned corporate body under the aegis of the Ministry of Railways, for the facilitation and promotion of intermodal transportation in the country. Following this decision, CONCOR was incorporated in March 1988.

Liberalization of the economy: International trade today serves as the bedrock for an increasingly interdependent global network of technology, investment and production. India realized it could grow fast only as part of the world, not in isolation; it must create an environment and framework that would provide strong impetus to exports.

Genesis: Containerization and intermodal transportation have emerged as the vehicle for efficient logistics arrangement. Slow and tardy, though, the development of containerization in India began when the first ISO container was brought to India's south-west coast, at Cochin port by an APL vessel on 27 November 1973. It was five years later that the first international container service was introduced on India-Australia corridor in September 1978. For as long as another decade intermodal transportation remained generally a mere concept. The slow development at India's ports was matched by even slower development of infrastructure for intermodal networks inland.

Indian Railways (IR) the pioneer: It goes to the credit of IR to have the foresight in the 1960s to realize the immense potential as well as benefits of cargo transported door-to-door through integrated intermodal arrangement. IR had in earlier years launched a rudimentary intermodal service for "smalls" or less than wagon load traffic through street collection and delivery service.

The gradual decline of railways in most of the industrialized countries had a lesson for IR, which too observed that it needed to think and act afresh for the fast dwindling general goods traffic, that as a rule was high revenue-yielding. Containerized intermodal transport was thus started in India as far back as 1966-1967 by IR with the transportation of domestic cargo in, what were known as Indian Railway Standard (IRS), containers. (Three IRS containers of 5-ton capacity each would be counted as equivalent to one ISO TEU). IR inducted 4.5-ton and 5-ton containers for carrying intracountry cargo between metropolitan cities. Not much progress could, however, be made to run unit trains of containers. Consistent with the then myopic view generally held, IR fell a prey to doing most operations in-house, all pre-carriage and post-carriage activities including collection and delivery of cargo, even all millwright activities for operating and maintaining cranes vehicles, and containers. IRS containers remained in use till 1994, although no separate accountal was made for them. They were subsumed in the overall throughput data after 1991-1992. Table 1 provides IRS container traffic and earnings by year.

Table 1. Traffic in (5-ton capacity) domestic containers

Year	Number of containers	Earnings (million rupee) Rs
1980-1981	43 649	NA
1981-1982	37 864	NA
1982-1983	36 173	NA
1983-1984	32 276	53.8
1984-1985	36 779	66.0
1985-1986	36 390	74.2
1986-1987	38 433	68.9
1987-1988	36 113	71.7
1988-1989	27 900	66.8
1989-1990	29 281	73.8
1990-1991	26 649	83.2
1991-1992	37 485	NA

Source: Commercial Directorate, Railway Board, Ministry of Railways, India.

Notes: Fiscal year: 1 April to 31 March of the following year.

Starting with an improvised ICD at Bangalore within the rail freight handling siding at the station, in August 1981, IR designated a few other similar ICDs at Anaparti, Coimbatore, Guntur, Guwahati, Ludhiana and Pragati Maidan (New Delhi). The first four among them provided the linkage for movement of containers to and from Cochin and Madras ports; ICD at Guwahati was linked to Calcutta and Haldia ports, primarily for tea exports; ICD at Delhi had its connectivity to Bombay port. In 1988-1989, the total container handling at these ICDs was of 43,065 TEU, a mere 8.7 per cent of the containers handled at the gateway ports.

Handling and transport of ISO containers from gateway ports to hinterland was started by IR in 1981-1982.   A 229 TEU throughput was achieved in the initial year.   This throughput level rose to 43,065 TEU in 1988-1989, by which time, domestic IRS container throughput had drastically reduced from the 1980-1981 peak of 14,549 TEU equivalent to 9,300 TEU equivalent. The share of container traffic in IR's total freight traffic in 1988-1989 was less than 0.2 per cent by volume.   Of a total IR's freight loading of 302 million tons, containerized traffic accounted for less than 0.5 million tons. International trade required more transit-time sensitivity and 'small-volume customer' care than what IR with its focus on large volumes of bulk commodities could provide.

I. CONCOR COMES INTO BEING

The fledgling CONCOR in its small way had an important task to manage change in India's logistics architecture.   It had its task laid out: spearhead the container revolution in the country, build and operate infrastructure linkages for rapid and accelerated inland penetration of containerized international trade traffic; develop and promote the use of ISO containers for intra-country domestic general goods, duly aggregate them for unit train operation on specified routes; develop technologies for optimal intermodal services including concepts of piggyback and roadrailer; provide pragmatic and technical knowhow consultancy and management services in the field of intermodal transportation, warehousing, management of terminals, packaging and palletisation, container leasing and repairs; and function as a model intermodal transport operator.

A string of dry ports

Set up with the objective of providing comprehensive integrated intermodal logistics support for India's international and domestic trade by way of direct door-to-door services, encompassing the flexibility of road transportation along with robust and economical unit train advantage of countrywide rail network, CONCOR moved about establishing a string of ICDs and container freight stations (CFSs).

The new gateway at Nhava Sheva near Mumbai steadily emerged as the main container terminal on the west coast linked to the sprawling hinterland in the western and central parts of the country as well as the northern and north-western region.   The gateway itself came to be the largest beneficiary of intermodal infrastructure, especially the CONCOR's flagship ICDs at Tughlakabad in Delhi and at Ludhiana in Punjab.

Rail and road links were established with six of the eleven major ports in the country, with dedicated container liner services between Delhi and the ports of Mumbai, Nhava Sheva, and Chennai. The linkages on the network incorporated all good features of road and rail, in fact, the best of road and rail together. CONCOR utilized extensive rail network for long hauls, while road vehicles were involved for door-to-door deliveries and short lead movements. Modal choice was dictated by the efficiencies and economies of transportation.

Within two years of taking over the business, CONCOR more than doubled its container handling from 52,084 TEU in 1989-1990 to 108,277 TEU at the close of 1991-1992. Of this, 95,782 TEU were export/import containers. Compared with the container handling at the then 11 major ports, projected at 669,000 TEU in 1990-1991, container handling in the hinterland continued to be low, at about 10-11 per cent. The changes in India's export-import basket, the rising share of manufactured and value-added export trades and of general cargoes in import trades constituting more than 70 per cent of total trade volumes, demanded greater sophistication in handling and transit that containerization represented. Figure 1 indicates the growing incidence of containerization in India's external trade in relation to the overall cargo volume handled at its gateway ports.

Figure 1. Total cargo and share of containers

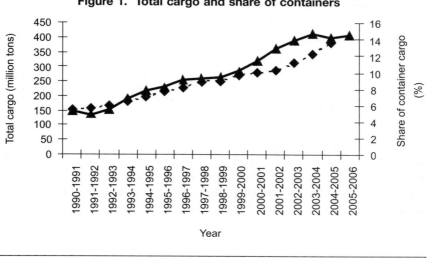

- - ◆ - - Total Cargo Traffic at Major Ports   ▲ Share of Container Cargo: %

Source: Indian Ports Association.

The extent of containerized cargo volumes handled at different ports depended on the requisite infrastructure facilities available. In respect of the share of containerized cargo in non-bulk general cargo, JNP has been in clear lead, in fact, serving almost as an exclusive container handling port followed by Chennai, Cochin, Kolkata and Tuticorin. Table 2 shows it in a nutshell.

Table 2. Volume of cargo at major ports in 2005-2006

Ports	Total cargo (million tons)	General cargo			Share of general cargo as per cent of total	Share of containerized cargo in general cargo (per cent)
		Others	Containerized	Total		
		(million tons)				
All major ports	423.42	68.98	61.83	130.81	30.90	47.30
Kolkata	10.81	2.49	3.23	5.72	52.90	56.50
Haldia	42.22	5.20	1.71	6.91	16.40	24.70
Visakhapatnam	55.80	8.84	2.63	9.47	17.00	27.80
Ennore	9.17	–	–	–	–	–
Chennai	47.25	8.58	11.76	20.34	43.00	57.80
Tuticorin	17.14	5.35	3.43	8.78	51.20	39.10
Cochin	13.94	0.88	2.54	3.42	24.50	74.30
New Mangalore	34.45	1.43	0.15	1.58	4.60	9.50
Mormugao	31.69	1.94	0.11	2.05	6.50	5.40
Mumbai	44.19	11.84	2.15	13.95	31.60	15.40
JNPT	37.75	1.48	33.78	35.26	93.40	95.80
Kandla	45.91	16.94	2.31	19.25	41.90	12.00
Paradip	33.11	4.03	0.05	4.08	12.30	1.20

Source: Indian Ports Association.

As CONCOR moved about, generating container culture and consciousness in the country, it had firm plans drawn up to increase the number of container terminals that in Phase I, by the end of the Eighth Five Year Plan (1992-1997), would cover most of the major trade centres in the country. Realizing that resources will always be difficult to come by, CONCOR chose to improvise and build in stages. It helped conserve resources, cut costs of operations and build speedily.

Trail-blazer

CONCOR rests on the firm foundation of essential countrywide infrastructure it has built and ancillary software of systems it has put in place.

While it has engendered the crucial intermodal milieu in the industry, concomitant institutional framework has simultaneously come up to help expand and sustain the practice. The first few years of CONCOR's existence were more than an ambitious agenda of action, which was necessary not just for targets to be achieved, but for its relatively new technology to take root in the country's industrial and logistics milieu. Other important features relevant to legal, financial, and claims and compensation issues, and electronic date interchange, required to be constantly kept in focus for best global practices and systems to be incorporated in India's procedural and policy framework.

With around 30 per cent of total containerized export-import cargo handled at India's ports being carried by CONCOR mostly by rail to and from a network of dry ports, it provides the gains and facility of integrated mobility technology to shippers in almost every nook and corner of the country. Although CONCOR must strive to increase the rail-borne container traffic from and to ports much beyond the current 30 per cent level, this share in the intermodal business is far higher than what has been achieved by, say, the two of the world's largest comparable railway systems in China and the Russian Federation.

Triggers qualitative changes

CONCOR has played a pioneering role in India for ushering in intermodal transportation of export-import trade. Intermodal transport infrastructure development fostered by CONCOR brought about far-reaching qualitative changes in the internationalization of production as well as to enable Indian industry and commerce to acquire the requisite competitive edge in terms of cost, quality and reliability. Around its ICDs and CFSs, regional production networks grow and expand. Spatial dispersal of economic activities follows; and improved access to inland centres of industry and trade helps spread the benefits of economic growth from the traditionally strong coastal areas around ports.

Together with new growth impulses arising around new inland centres of industrial and commercial activity, an environment of competition as much as integration of services helps transaction costs to be lowered and time to be saved.

ICDs and CFSs as dry ports make a tangible contribution to growth, directly, through reduced transaction costs and, indirectly, through productivity gains as entrepreneurs organise their manufacturing and distribution more efficiently. CONCOR's ICDs and CFSs provide facilities for cross-border trade to prosper in hinterland with linkages to gateway ports.

CONCOR devised its business strategy to be in harmony in the trinity of time, space and motion. As its core business of a carrier, a terminal operator and logistics operator, CONCOR pursued the essence and purport of intermodalism with the primacy of rail transit, road services being utilized mostly in the form of supplementary services to provide door-to-door linkages. Wherever it is operationally or economically a superior option, road has been used as an alternative to rail.

Essentially customer-driven

The CONCOR testament desired every customer to be served for an abiding relationship to recognize the different needs of its customers. Its customers were its partners. It strove to provide them a continuous stream of ideas and innovations to make their business operations efficient and profitable. CONCOR began providing integrated transport services, bringing advantages of containerization to the shippers' doorsteps – unitization, reduced handling, free from damages and pilferages, facility of customs inspection, direct supervision of stuffing/destuffing of cargoes, leading also to better stowage and consequent gains in ocean freight costs. With the terminals working as one-stop, single-window facilities and an optimal mix of road-cum-rail services from factory to port, a complete service package was offered.

Cost and quality primary concern

CONCOR maintained a commitment to cost consciousness. The realization that high costs inevitably got passed on to the users, rendering country's products uncompetitive, impelled the CONCOR executives to analyse and minimize cost of services as an ongoing exercise.

Prior to CONCOR coming into being, the makeshift ICDs were being operated by IR and point-to-point lumpsum rate had been fixed for transport of containers from and to ports. There were separate rates for different streams/routes worked out on the basis of fully distributed unit costs of the zonal railways with a margin of profit. While taking over the then existing ICDs from IR in 1989, CONCOR persuaded the former to fix a flat rate per TEU per km payable by CONCOR, without relating it to each stream or route. Weighted average cost of all streams of traffic was worked out, and a flat rate per km was derived; a 15 per cent rebate on the cost so determined was allowed for services not rendered by IR (documentation and other terminal services, marketing, etc.); and a 20 per cent profit for IR was added to such rebate-adjusted cost.

Tariffs and terms

CONCOR also implemented a simplified tariff system as a package, covering most of the generic service, inclusive of terminal handling at both ends, lift-on, lift-off of boxes, positioning thereof, documentation as well as transportation. It was essential that it settled with IR all such important commercial and operational details, for it to function with its own identity and flexibility.

Towards this objective, IR would be working as an agent of CONCOR for the services to be specified in the agreement. The charge by way of terminal costs was to be excluded from these tariffs, as the operations would be conducted by CONCOR. The gross weight of two ordinary 4-wheeler wagons was more than that of a flat freight car containing two TEUs, leading to the average cost for haulage of the container per km being less than that for conventional wagons. Economies of scale would accrue to IR, if traffic was offered in train loads, and as such, CONCOR insisted that consideration be given to it for having a competitive edge to establish itself in the field of intermodal transport.

In fact, the Railway Fare and Freight Committee appointed by the Ministry of Railways further recommended in their report in December 1993 that

> "The principles for fixation of rates for containerized cargo or for that matter any general goods cargo requiring multimodal transport, will have to be different from the principles adopted for fixation of standard commodity rates for bulk traffic."

The Committee maintained

> "A distinction should be made in the rate for a block train and a piecemeal flat. Cost of marshalling should be deducted in the case of former, and a lower rate be charged. We have recommended 5 to 11 per cent reduction in train load rates from wagon load rates. We recommend that block trains of containers should be charged at 5 per cent lower than wagon load rates."

To keep it simple and slim

In its freight charge on the basis of per TEU km, CONCOR has opted for a simplified tariff structure, levying a virtual freight all kind (FAK) irrespective of the commodity in the box. It has also kept container and cargo handling charges standardized. A composite and consolidated charge is quoted for most of the common services including terminal handling charges at the ICD and the gateway together with haulage cost for rail transit of the container.

CONCOR's Inland Way Bill (IWB) covered road-cum-rail haulage, although the undefined liability regime and the uncertainty with regard to settlement of claims remained an area of concern. IWB signified CONCOR's abiding urge to simplify documentation sans bureaucratic rigmarole.

Low cost model

CONCOR recognized that deployment of resources, both human and technological, must generate high efficiency and productivity. Lofty, lumpy investments were eschewed; instead, sights were generally set on small-improvised facilities, to begin with, involving minimal expenditure and timeframe. ICDs set up at Sabarmati in Ahmedabad, Chinchwad in Pune, Sanatnagar in Hyderabad, Shalimar in Calcutta were examples of this corporate thrust. That enabled CONCOR to have these schemes and projects, long awaited for years, put on the ground in a matter of a few months. The response from trade and industry was equally encouraging, so also the help and cooperation from the relevant regulatory departments and agencies, particularly Customs.

CONCOR followed a deliberate policy of keeping capital costs low initially. Facilities were built in stages on a modular pattern as traffic picked up after the setting up of the interim-phase improvised terminals to provide the basic facilities speedily. Subsequently, it proceeded with unrelenting vigour to develop integrated full-fledged ICDs. At the same time, old terminals and depots were regularly strengthened; more linkages between the country's ports were established. The idea at CONCOR was a simple one, "fat birds don't fly": for them, it was so much more important to soar, not just fly. There was no sticking to a routine, no standard procedures, no frontiers drawn at individual desks and work windows.

CONCOR has adopted a lean and functional management structure (outlined in the chart below), to be constantly reviewed and revamped according to the needs and exigencies of business.

Figure 2. CONCOR's management organization

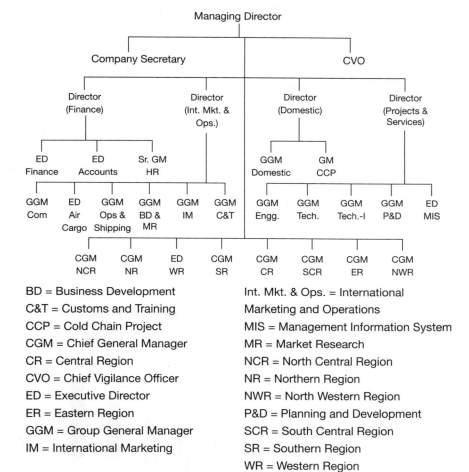

BD = Business Development
C&T = Customs and Training
CCP = Cold Chain Project
CGM = Chief General Manager
CR = Central Region
CVO = Chief Vigilance Officer
ED = Executive Director
ER = Eastern Region
GGM = Group General Manager
IM = International Marketing

Int. Mkt. & Ops. = International
Marketing and Operations
MIS = Management Information System
MR = Market Research
NCR = North Central Region
NR = Northern Region
NWR = North Western Region
P&D = Planning and Development
SCR = South Central Region
SR = Southern Region
WR = Western Region

II. A BLUE CHIP COMPANY

CONCOR has been maintaining a steady growth in its turnover; it has been more than doubled during the last five years, from Rs 11.10 billion in 2000-2001 to Rs 24.89 billion in 2005-2006. It has kept a lean organizational structure, with its employees' cost within 2 per cent of total expenditure. Its financial health is further reflected through the net worth of Rs 20.91 billion, and liquidity ratio of 2.47 and no debt in its balance sheet.

When the loss-sustaining public sector undertaking was common in the country, CONCOR closed its very first year of operations on a high note. It posted a pre-tax profit of Rs 10.04 million. It gained the confidence to sail afloat, although investments would be high. CONCOR is designated a *mini-ratna* (a tiny scintillating jewel) among India's public sector undertakings, an acknowledged blue chip, hailed as a new genre of lean and nimble, customer-driven corporate entity in the public sector.

Steadily moving on a high growth path consistently, in the range of 13 to 15 per cent annually, CONCOR has handsomely contributed to the shareholders' wealth. It started with authorized capital of Rs 1 billion and paid up capital of Rs 650 million; 37 per cent of its equity share capital has subsequently been disinvested, the balance 63 per cent share is held by the Government of India. Three tranches of divestment took place during 1994-1995, 1995-1996 and 1998-1999. The major private sector shareholders are foreign institutional investors (27.1 per cent), mutual funds and Unit Trust of India (4.67 per cent), banks and financial institutions (1.95 per cent), and the balance is held by non-resident Indians and other individuals. Financial performance of CONCOR is shown in figures 3 and 4 and in table 3.

Figure 3. Gross profit and dividend paid (crores of rupee)

(1 crore = 10 million)

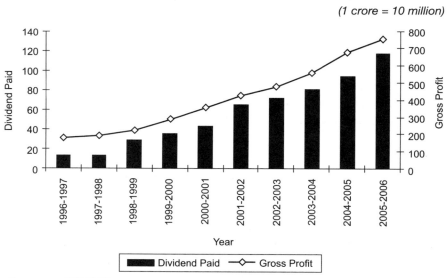

Source: CONCOR.

Figure 4. Earning per share of Rs 10

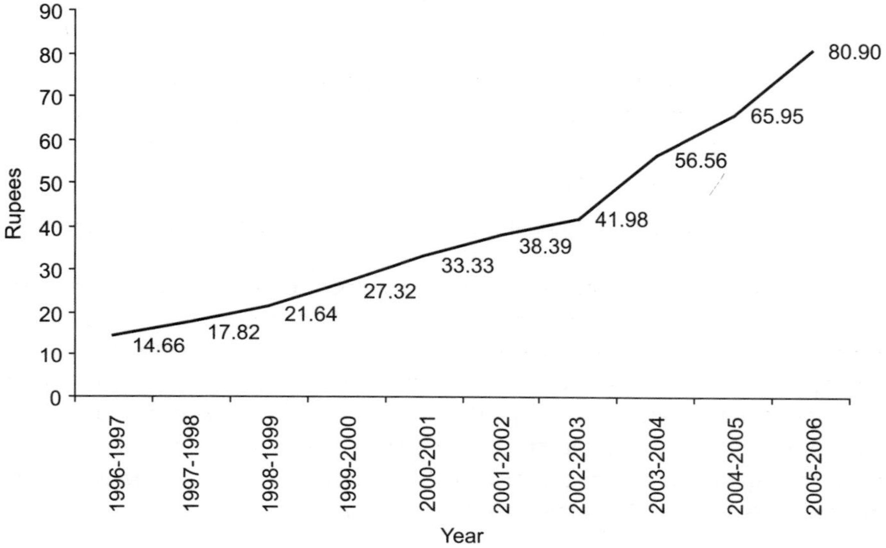

Source: CONCOR.

Table 3. Some salient financial indices

Per cent

	2002-2003	2003-2004	2004-2005	2005-2006
Return on capital employed	38.83	36.74	38.05	34.64
Return on equity	39.32	37.03	35.87	32.15
Return on fixed assets	27.77	30.66	27.85	29.31

Source: CONCOR.

III. CUSTOMER FOCUS AND INNOVATIVE URGE

New ground was broken and several initiatives brought in, e.g., direct stuffing of goods in containers straight from the road vehicle without first being unloaded and inspected by Customs. Likewise, the Central Excise staff posted for other regulatory functions in the factory supervised stuffing of containers and sealed them on behalf of Customs. This proved to be an important element in progressively increasing the factory stuffing/destuffing of export/import containers, thereby helping door-to-door intermodal transport gains accruing to trade. As a logical follow up of the above line of business, CONCOR has gone into:

- Mini-bridging of import containers from port to port by rail, with the objective of helping ships avoid calling at multiple ports within India.

- Bonded warehousing for long-term storage of import cargo, thus enabling fast release of import containers which, in turn, improved productivity of CONCOR's terminals as well as of the shipping lines.

- Addition of domestic containerized rail transport in its business.

Another cost-effective ingenuous scheme has been the institutionaliza-tion of road-chassis system; for instance, at Moradabad and Panipat, the former an important node for handicrafts and the latter for textile made-ups, empty containers from ICD at Delhi are taken on trailers, export cargo Customs-cleared and stacked in the warehouse in advance being directly stuffed into containers, while still on chassis, and the sealed containers move back to the rail container complex at Delhi all in a matter of few hours for onward dispatch to gateway port by an express block liner train.

Improvisations and innovations

CONCOR emphasized a commitment to the concept of productivity, economy, improvisation, and innovation. The concept of port side container terminal (PSCT) is an instance. Conceived and developed by CONCOR, a PSCT was commissioned in March 1991 at Tondiarpet, within 6 km from the port of Chennai. Wadi Bander came up the following month across the way from Bombay port. Much the same way, other PCSTs added a new dimension to container handling.

PSCTs complement the facilities offered by premier container handling ports, particularly the Chennai port on the east coast and the Nhava Sheva and Bombay ports on the west coast. The PSCTs or near-dock terminals or off-dock container centres constituted extremely cost-effective infrastructure providing virtual extension to the respective ports. They served as intermodal hubs concomitant to quayside operations, facilitating quick dispersal of import containers from ports, and efficient aggregation of export containers for timely loading on to vessels, and relieving congestion and reducing strain on the port infrastructure. The concept further facilitated the rail landbridge development to link specialized port hubs between the east coast and the west coast.

Ever new initiatives

CONCOR also planned to provide an answer to chronic congestion and bottlenecks of air cargo clearance of exports, particularly garments and leather products. Cargo congestion at important airports like Chennai, Delhi and Mumbai had been endemic, particularly during the busy season (November to March), when exports of garments and leather products attained their peak during the year. CONCOR's emphasis was on cost effective and speedy transit of Indian exports. For readymade garments and leather shoes, for example, it offered a specially designed composite package of logistics services. For expeditious aggregation and transit, specific days were nominated for carting of cargo prior to the container for the destination being stuffed and dispatched. The transit time was guaranteed by CONCOR, for which detailed logistics arrangements were finalized with Railways, ports and specific ocean carriers. The total logistics costs in the arrangement devised by CONCOR were no more than 30 per cent of the costs incurred by exporters in sending the cargo by air.

CONCOR believed in quality in everything they did, from loading containers, to filling forms, and answering phone calls – it was its way of putting the customer first. It was realized that CONCOR's success would revolve not around its terminals, offices, facilities, depots, centres or computers but on how well, efficiently, pleasantly, innovatively, the specific needs and requirements of each customer were met. Its commitment was concentrated in individuals in as large a team as to handle any comprehensive challenge and as small to be most personalized.

The most important task CONCOR set for itself was to ensure the quality of service – guaranteed transits – to link with specified sailings; composite customized packages from door-to-door; innovative solutions to customer problems; prompt efficient service, eliminating excessive documentation and procedural wrangles. CONCOR also aimed at running exclusive liner trains with fixed formations, published time tables, advanced reservation of container space, and rail-cum-road transportation of cargo from door-to-door.

IV. BLENDING SYNERGIES:
PUBLIC PRIVATE PARTNERSHIP

In regard to current widespread clamour for PPP (public-private partnership), CONCOR has in essence been its ardent advocate and practitioner. It has steadfastly joined hands with a number of private sector as well as public sector entities in order to blend the synergies and strengths for optimal advantage, cost reduction and efficiency enhancement.

Several *avant garde* combinations for PPP projects have been executed to harness commonality of interests for intermodal business. For the setting up of satellite CFSs, participation of agencies like the state and central warehousing corporations and those in the private sector was sought at locations where they had appropriate warehousing infrastructure available. For the interim-phase of development, cargo destuffing of import containers, customs inspection and delivery was envisaged at some of the customs-bonded warehouses of these agencies, e.g., at Ahmedabad, Amritsar, Hyderabad, Jalandhar, Ludhiana and Pune.

Private entrepreneurs were invited and encouraged to join hands with CONCOR in different spheres on mutually acceptable terms, for instance, in providing capital and trained manpower for handling equipment (cranes, trucks, forklifts, etc.), at its ICDs and CFSs, maintenance facilities, and terminal operations. Besides, CONCOR proposed to let the private operators handle on contract/under franchise all transport of containers and cargo by road between the satellite CFSs and the rail-fed ICDs, and between ICDs/CFSs and shippers' premises.

Several participatory models

Its strategy of expanding business horizons by diversifying in allied areas by way of alliances and joint ventures has been continued unabated, for example, its joint venture partnership with major shipping lines at strategic locations. At Dadri, near Greater Noida, in the vicinity of Delhi, it has joint ventures with 49 per cent equity participation with four shipping lines: Maersk, APL, CMA CGM, and Transworld to develop CFSs. It has also entered into development and operation of the third container terminal at JNP, through a joint venture (JV) with Maersk, with 26 per cent equity contribution. The terminal with a capacity to handle 1.3 million TEU became operational in March 2006. Another JV it has entered into with Dubai Port World with 15 per cent equity contribution to develop a container transhipment port at Vallarpadam in Cochin.

CONCOR has joined hands with others through a revenue sharing model, e.g., with Hindustan Aeronautics Limited at Bangalore to develop facilities for airfreight of export cargo. Similar ventures at Nasik and Goa have huge potential to export fruits, vegetables and other agricultural products.

A landmark has been achieved by starting coastal shipping in association with Seaways Limited and started container movement from Phillaur in Punjab to Chittagong in Bangladesh via Kolkata port. CONCOR has commenced cold atmosphere (CA) storage facility near Delhi at an estimated cost of Rs 1 billion, for which CONCOR has launched Fresh & Healthy Enterprise, its 100 per cent subsidary. To begin with, it proposes to procure apples from Shimla during the season, transport them in reefer containers to Delhi and stock them in CA store to be released during the off-season. The forward end integration with market has been done with a number of retail outlets in the national capital region.

A major growth strategy for both international and domestic businesses involves the use of the 'hub and spoke' system to serve the customer at his doorstep, while optimizing the internal logistics chain within the organization. In an effort to move from being a service integrator, CONCOR is also moving towards becoming a third party logistics (3PL) service provider by expanding the core business into areas such as warehousing, auto carriage on rail, refrigerated cargo storage and movement, and a large number of other value added services. It has set its sight high for expanding its business horizons by ingeniously diversifying in allied areas and has forged strategic alliances and joint ventures.

Another instance of evolving collaboration among various players keen to eke a share in the burgeoning intermodal business is a joint venture recently forged between CONCOR and Gateway Rail Freight Pvt. Ltd., a subsidiary of Gateway Distriparks, to construct and operate a rail-linked container terminal at Garhi Harsaru near Gurgaon in close proximity of Delhi. The joint venture particularly targets the high potential of double-stack container carrying train operation between the National Capital Region and the west coast container terminals at Gujarat ports of Mundra and Pipavav.

V. OPTIMAL MODAL MIX

Helping IR face increasing competition from road, and gain rail share in the niche market of value added manufactures, CONCOR has pursued a strategic concept of 'hub and spoke' operations with recourse to road or short haul rail shuttle services within defined catchment areas. Some hubs like the ICD at Tughlakabad are fed by several satellite locations such as Panipat or even Gwalior, until traffic steadily builds up and justifies running a scheduled service from the satellite facility itself, as was done initially in the case of Ludhiana and Moradabad, which started out as remote locations linked to the hub terminal at Tughlakabad. For domestic cargo as well, 'hub and spoke' movements allow better utilization of resources by way of long lead services generated on the basis of short lead traffic collections using road and rail shuttle services. Unbridled by any dogmatic modal preference, CONCOR uses high speed heavy duty Volvo trucks to provide efficient road connectivity between, say, ICD, Bangalore and the gateway port of Chennai. Also, bonded trucking services for less than container load (LCL) export consolidation from, and delivery of LCL imports to, hinterland locations have been introduced between Chennai and many major industrial centres in southern India.

With road linkages between the satellite CFSs owned and managed by CONCOR, as well as most of the other CFSs, the aim was to provide a comprehensive network to cover most of the major trade centres in the country, which constituted salient nodes for production and distribution of export-import goods. Most of the CFSs and all ICDs owned by CONCOR, together with the road/rail linkages it provides, enables it to offer a complete service package unlike what can be obtained in many other countries.

VI. ICDs AND CFSs

CONCOR ICDs provide single window facility to customers for intermodal cargo transport by way of cargo aggregation and storage, palletisation, container stuffing, customs clearance, truck and trailer parking, banking and office space for customers' agents/employees regularly working at CONCOR terminals. Right from its inception, CONCOR visualized the satellite centres – CFSs or Trade Development Centres (TDCs) – to be export promotion and trade growth centres, extending myriad infrastructural support to the shipper. CONCOR ICDs extend the following additional facilities:

- Online information and container tracking
- Container repair and cleaning facilities
- Cargo palletisation, strapping, lashing/choking, etc.
- Fumigation of cargo/containers
- Door delivery/pick-up of containerized cargo
- Container/cargo survey
- Pre-deposit accounts
- Flexible payment arrangements
- Provision of reefer facilities

CONCOR's most important and biggest ICD at Tughlakabad, New Delhi, was commissioned on 1 September 1993. Its annual throughput exceeds 500,000 TEU. Another large unit is the mega terminal at Dadri (near Delhi), which, when working to full capacity, is likely to be the world's largest container terminal. A unique feature of the Dadri ICD is that it houses independent CFSs, joint ventures between CONCOR and renowned global shipping and container terminal operators. The terminal is a new State-of-the-art inland container terminal covering 110 hectare of land. Phase I envisages annual handling of 500,000 TEU with enhancement of the capacity to 1 million TEU per year.

CONCOR's current pan-India network aggregates 58 ICDs and CFSs among an overall total of 120 of such facilities all over the country set up and operated by various public and private entities. Most of the CONCOR facilities are located in the states of Andhra, Gujarat, Maharashtra, Punjab, Rajsthan, Tamil Nadu, Uttar Pradesh and West Bengal. Four more terminals are under construction – at Suranasi (Jalandhar), Khemli (Udaipur), Gurgaon and Sonepat.

A steady upward incline in CONCOR's throughput cumulatively at all its terminals is seen in Figure 5. No doubt, the progress in case of domestic container business suggests a lot to be desired.

Figure 5. CONCOR throughput: TEU

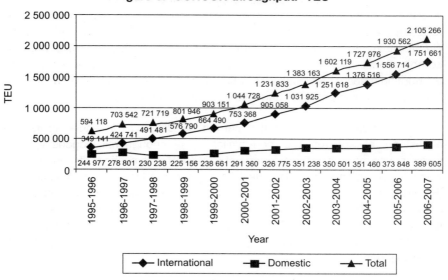

Source: CONCOR.

Ten of CONCOR's ICDs, largest in terms of throughput, namely, Tughlakabad (New Delhi), Dhandari Kalan (Ludhiana), Dadri (Greater Noida), Sabarmati (Ahmedabad), Dronagiri Node (near JNP), Whitefield (Bangalore), New Mulund (Mumbai), Tondiarpet (Chennai), Madras Harbour and Nagpur, account for over 70 per cent of total throughput CONCOR achieves at all its ICDs and CFSs. There is also a sharp imbalance in regional spread: the western and north-western regions account for 68 per cent of all export-import containers handled by CONCOR; the southern sector has a share of 25 per cent; and the eastern region is left with a meager share of 7 per cent.

VII. HOME TRADE: FOR HIGH GROWTH RATE

CONCOR added a new dimension to home trade. As it went about its schemes strengthening its infrastructure for an effective contribution to the growth of country's cross-border trade, it planned to simultaneously bring about a reorientation of production-distribution management of domestic trade cargo. The growing sophistication of India's industry necessitated commensurate infrastructural support. The terminals at the four major metropolitan conurbations – Delhi, Bombay, Madras and Calcutta – formed the cornerstones of CONCOR's expanding domestic network.

By way of efficient logistics support all the way from factory to market, it constantly experimented for raw material components and subassemblies to reach the production centres. CONCOR even organized round-trip closed-circuit movement, utilizing the most cost-effective time-sensitive rail-road combinations. For it, logistics arrangements meant better inventory and distribution management with just-in-time deliveries, which would go a long way in giving the Indian producer and supplier a competitive edge.

Domestic container traffic carried by CONCOR in earlier years was almost entirely the result of non-availability of enough rail wagons with IR. Cement was more than three-fourths of CONCOR's domestic traffic and the rest was pig iron and sponge iron, wheat flour and miscellaneous commodities. As IR resumed covered wagon purchases and eliminated wagon shortages, further increase in CONCOR's domestic traffic in commodities like cement, steel, and foodgrains was reversed. The loss of traffic in the heavy commodities was compensated by actively marketing for containerized movement of aggregated general goods.

The potential for containerization of home trade cargo is immense. As Indian industry and agriculture get more diversified and sophisticated and logistics of efficient inland transportation significantly begin to determine the production-distribution matrix, containerization of domestic trade will no longer remain a choice but will become a necessity. CONCOR perceived a great potential inherent in this development. It initiated a dialogue with important shipping lines and international leasing companies in order that the inflow of empty containers was maintained for containerized export cargoes to move from inland dry ports like Delhi. These empty containers could be tapped for carriage of intra-country traffic. In response, several shipping lines joined hands. Special express trains carrying empty containers were run from Wadi Bunder to Delhi, Calcutta, and Guwahati, from Kandla port to Delhi as also from Calcutta to Delhi, many of them carrying domestic cargo.

CONCOR has a fleet of over 12,000 owned and leased ISO containers for the use of its domestic customers. These are not just general purposes boxes, but include various special types of containers. Containers of varying shapes and sizes for domestic business have been deployed, their use being determined by the commodity stuffed in them.

Recently CONCOR introduced a live-in forty foot container which is a special container developed for personnel to escort the movement of sensitive cargo. It provides accommodation for personnel, say, for escorting sensitive goods in container trains as well as during escort's stay at terminals. It has up to eight bunk beds to accommodate 16 people and is equipped with facilities like toilet, pantry, coolers, electric power generator, etc.

VIII. TECHNOLOGY SUPPORT

Hardware

Although rail-borne container transit in the initial years relied on make-shift container carrying wagons within the IR fleet and even inducted some general purpose wagons to cater for peaks in demand, CONCOR has acquired state-of-the-art high speed container carrying flats capable of running at 100 km/hour. Six thousand such wagons are already deployed, while additional stock is constantly added to the fleet to cope with the growth in business and to replace the old outworn stock. CONCOR also purchased some 1,300 freight cars from IR, which have since been upgraded and retrofitted for improved service and better transit times.

Generally following a policy of distributive partnerships on the basis of comparative strength and specialization conducive to overall economies and efficiency in operations, CONCOR involves competent specialized agencies and operators for container handling as well as transport at its terminals. Nevertheless, at selected facilities such as its flagship ICD at Tughlakabad, CONCOR owns, operates and maintains an array of its own state-of-the-art sophisticated equipment, including a rail mounted gantry, rubber tyre gantries and reach stackers.

Software

With considerable advance in the information technology (IT) domain, CONCOR has been in the forefront of technology used to enhance efficiency, cost effectiveness and customer satisfaction. Since the Container and Cargo Logistics System (CCLS) went online at ICD at Tughlakabad in 1994, CONCOR has set up a company-wide satellite-based intranet. It has four Enterprise Resource Packages (ERP) systems in place, namely, Export Terminal Management System (ETMS), Domestic Terminal Management System (DTMS), Human Resources and Payroll Management System (RMCO), and Financial Management System (Oracle financials).

Customers need information and documentation systems for booking, tracking, paying, clearing cargo accurately and expeditiously. Computerized container control has become an integral part of CONCOR operations. CONCOR terminals are integrated by intermodal connections and logistics supported by a management information system. The VSAT-based network has been extended and now covers 54 locations. The Terminal Management Systems have been implemented using that VSAT-based network that links field locations/regional offices and the corporate office. The web-enabled system through a web server provides answers to queries from customers. A customer feedback system has also been implemented on its website. This has enabled CONCOR to constantly evaluate its performance and take corrective actions on complaints and feedback. An e-filing facility on commercial system (CCLS) at ICD Tughlakabad has been introduced for customers to file their documents electronically.

Radio data terminals (RDTs) are being used at the ICDs at Tughlakabad and Dadri for online container tracking and entry of unloading/loading of containers on to wagons. Interface software helps in automatic updating of entries through RDTs into CCLS and ETMS database for international operations. RDTs are also interfaced with DTMS, thereby enabling users to query the system either through LAN or Web to get the latest status and location of a container in the CONCOR network.

CONCOR's own web server provides web interface for customers to access information regarding their shipments. Additionally, an integrated track and trace system on CONCOR website provides container tracking details, train summaries and current train running status.

Customers can search details of trains dispatched from a particular station to any destination. There is a further link on train number, which, on clicking, displays the complete train summary details including all the containers loaded on that train, wagons number, container size and container status.

IX. EMERGING COMPETITION

It is believed that generally 40 per cent of port traffic originates from and terminates at places within 300 km from the port, the rest 60 per cent is traffic for the hinterland. The share of CONCOR and other similar agencies that may come up in the future is about 60 per cent of the total containerized international traffic handled at ports. The room for increasing CONCOR's traffic is, therefore ample and, if CONCOR can add capacity and provide transport linkages between ports and hinterland of acceptable standard at competitive prices, its international traffic can grow substantially. Its export and import traffic has been maintaining sustainable growth over the years both in terms of originating loading as well as handling of containers.

The possibilities of growth in container traffic in domestic sector are also bright. Logistics parks and large cargo hubs become a necessity, as large retail chains would generate the demand for professionally managed cargo delivery systems.

With fourteen more players coming in this field, the organization finds itself in a competitive environment. With its formidable infrastructure across the country, consistent growth profile in the past, trained manpower and dedicated customer base, it is confident to maintain its growth rate in the future.

CONCOR's steady increase in intermodal business has attracted a large number of corporates including a few of the important global operators joining Indian companies. Triggered by a discreet move by IR to let other private sector enterprises to operate container trains in addition to the hitherto exclusive operator that CONCOR has been, the new entrants in the business should help augment the much needed capacity for container transportation, which is projected to witness exponential growth in demand.

The fifteen container licencees (including CONCOR) are classified in two categories: (i) a registration fee of Rs 500 million allows operators to offer containerized services across the country for both export-import and domestic traffic; and (ii) a Rs 100 million fee will allow operators to move domestic containerized traffic across the country, but international containerized traffic can be moved only from specified ports.

X. FUTURE: CHALLENGING AND EXCITING

A clear plateauing of CONCOR's share in container traffic at the country's ports at a level of 30-31 per cent for the last many years (as indicated in figure 6 below) warrants a time-bound strategy for it as much as IR to expeditiously and steadily expand the capacity on selected routes. To some extent, the new entrants (licencees) will help by way of providing additional wagons and inland terminals. However, the saturated rail routes cry out for quick and ingenious solutions.

Figure 6. Port throughput and CONCOR's share

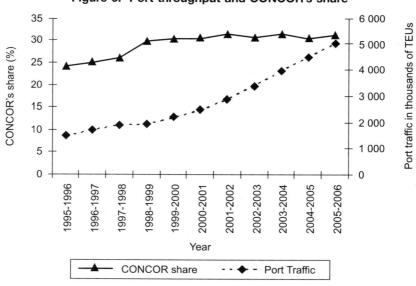

Source: Indian Ports Association.

Whereas containerization of India's export-import trade grew at 14 per cent per year during the period 1992-2005 in comparison to 7 per cent growth in overall cargo volumes handled at India's major ports, there are deficiencies that have shown up. With the national economy recording an annual increase of over 8 per cent in recent years, there is a clear need to expeditiously put in place additional wherewithal of container handling facilities at ports with appropriate linkages to hinterlands, develop efficient infrastructure on the east coast where the share of container business has been a paltry 7-8 per cent, substantially enhance capacity of rail and road networks to and from major container handling ports, further improve productivity and efficiency at ports, streamline procedures and regulations with optimal utilization of IT, and reduce rates and charges for different facilities through the logistics chain. An unrelenting commitment has to be maintained to weave a genuine and preemptive concern for customer care at all levels.

In the context of an overwhelming share of container business originating from, and terminating in places around Delhi and in adjoining states in the northern and north western parts of India, the greenfield "intermediate" ports along the Gujarat coast – particularly Mundra and Pipavav – may emerge as the most promising gateways, more so because these ports are connected by rail without overhead electric wires, which allows double-stack container trains to operate. Rail track distances from these ports to northern and north-western India are also shorter than the erstwhile direct route from JNP to these centres. In a rapidly evolving environment, new private sector port projects like Dhamra on the east coast – between Kolkata and Paradip as also the port at Rewas near New Mumbai hold a great potential and promise.

The proposed dedicated rail freight corridors for west-north and east-north streams of traffic will take a few years to materialize. Some viable interim solution is indeed of paramount importance. The competitive participation by private sector aspirants in rail transport of containers will help, but they have to go about developing inland terminals and procure wagon fleet. In fact, acute rail transport shortage will be exacerbated on critical corridors such as the one along the west coast between Delhi and Mumbai.

In view of the steadily rising volumes and long distances for them to traverse, rail transport is a clear choice for at least 50 per cent of the containers handled at Indian ports. A great opportunity that double stack container train operation can provide needs to be grasped to make a great success of it most expeditiously.

India has a vast potential to explore and exploit intermodal logistics for domestic cargo. CONCOR has been able to do but a modest job so far. A great deal still needs to be done. IR will need to take a long-range view for facilitating large logistics hubs by way of freight villages, logistics or distriparks to come up in railway complexes for intermodal services for domestic cargo to

Figure 7. Indian Railways' double stack train

Courtesy: CONCOR.

register an exponential growth. It is in IR's interest to frame its tariffs for these services in a long-term perspective. These services have the potential to alter IR's business profile towards container carrying trains operated at lower tariffs proving the proverbial golden goose, besides yielding other economic and environmental gains to the country.

Terminal handling of inbound and outbound air cargo commenced by CONCOR in close conjunction with some airlines at a couple of locations can expand. Air cargo does need considerable logistics support. Allied with it, rail-based intermodal support to get a good share of express freight should yield good gains. This segment will call for same day or next day delivery and a product faster than road and cheaper than air.

With a beginning already made by way of its own subsidiary Fresh and Healthy Enterprises, CONCOR will hopefully emerge as a major player in cold chain logistics for exports and imports of different commodities and products. It will aim to be a dominant trend setter to wrest a lion's share of intracountry traffic in fruits and vegetables. It may be mentioned that IR have traditionally run onion and potato specials, mango and banana trains, and also special vans for fish and poultry.

Now with the container handling terminals at ports being developed almost entirely in PPP mode, there is a steady confidence built up that ports by themselves may not be much of an impediment. No doubt, ports need to cut down delays and costs. It is also essential that some of Indian ports develop a critical mass instead of diffusing the effort at many of them.

XI. CONCLUSION

In India, CONCOR was the pioneer in its field and has thus far enjoyed a virtual monopoly. It started off with all the qualities of a leader – breadth of vision, meticulous planning, cost and quality consciousness, and care of the needs of the customer. But as the competition gets into the act, its leadership is going to be challenged. It is time for it to think bold and fresh, contemplate pragmatic collaboration with global liner services and container terminal operators, among other things, to forge alliances for developing cross-border intermodal logistics services across the region and subregions, for land bridging of containerized freight for the SAARC region, and for developing a maritime regional hub on the country's east coast. CONCOR may well also explore the potential of coastal shipping and inland waterways in partnership with appropriate players, and mount a really ambitious project to establish nodal logistics centres for domestic containerized cargo with value added services.

Logistics has acquired a new significance today as an essential and important segment of management and intermodal has emerged as its cornerstone. There is an awakening world over in favour of intermodalism. Asia and the Pacific needs to commit itself to maximizing intermodal linkages across the region. For countries like India and China, intermodalism signifies an undisputed primacy and potential to be nurtured and promoted, especially in the context of continental distances and huge volumes involved. It is expected that intermodal transportation with preponderance of rail will constitute the bulwark of integrated logistics support system for India's industry and agriculture in the future.

CONTAINER TRANSPORTATION BY RAIL IN THE RUSSIAN FEDERATION

Petr Baskakov*

ABSTRACT

Structural reforms are being undertaken by the Russian Railways (RZD). One of the important elements of reform measures refers to segregation of container transportation from transportation of other freight and positioning it as a competitive business segment. RZD has established TransContainer, a subsidiary for this purpose. The progress that TransContainer has made so far and the improvement measures that are being implemented including strategies that have been taken by the subsidiary for its growing business development are discussed in the article.

The containerized cargo transportation plays a special role in the worldwide exchange of goods as it allows direct shipment of commodities without any transhipment. Being a secure and cost-effective technology, containerization facilitates to a maximum extent the intercontinental flow of goods shipped by a combination of land and water transport. A brief glance at the evolving processes of containerization worldwide shows that their practical implementation requires new approaches to management that can diversify business and operations of various types of transport, the railway transport in particular.

The Russian Federation is one of the largest players involved in the global exchange of goods. Occupying over 30 per cent of Eurasia, the country is a natural landbridge providing transport links between Europe and Asia. This is particularly important in view of the fact that the volume of trade between East Asia and Europe is rapidly growing and container transport by rail has the promise of providing an attractive alternative to the existing sea route for this traffic.

---

*   General Director, TransContainer, Russian Federation.

Until recently the functions assigned to domestic railways were those of a mere transporter, which, to a certain extent, legally impeded development of other types of its operations and activities. The need for adaptation of the rail transport business to market mechanisms has become apparent to capitalize on the inherent advantages of rail transport in carrying large volumes of cargo over a long distance. In this situation, the containerized cargo transportation with the application of a wide variety of logistics technologies and segregation and consolidation of this type of transport operations from other types of freight carriage under a new business model is a starting point in its adaptation process to market mechanism that can utilize the natural advantages of the rail transport.

Given the current trend of development in the transportation industry, it is the rail transport that will form the foundation of the Russian container transport logistics and will play an important role as the national business integrator. The basic arrangements for accomplishing this task include the segregation of containerized cargo transportation from other commodities and placing it in a competitive business segment. It also requires determining the forms of consolidation of the container transportation business with due consideration of the specificities of the Russian railway transport system and ways of its integration with the international transport system.

An analysis showed that such arrangements for a new business model could be implemented only through a structural reform of the railway transport system in the Russian Federation. However, there is no universal standard solution for structural arrangements and management of containerized cargo transportation. Also, no typical method for the segregation of container transportation from transportation of other commodities and positioning it as a competitive business segment is available. The areas of possible restructuring depend on the initial conditions, the specificities of the legal and regulatory regimes, and the specific features of the sector under restructuring.

Accordingly, the segregation of containerized cargo transportation from transportation of other commodities and positioning it as a competitive business segment has become one of the important elements of the current structural reforms of the Russian Railways (RZD). As a result of these efforts, Russian Railways established a subsidiary – the Center for Cargo Container Traffic, TransContainer as an Open Joint-Stock Company. The organizational structure of the company is shown in figure 1. According to the new arrangement, the necessary assets (primarily container and railcar fleets) and container terminals/sites, where the flows of containers shipped by all types of transport start and end, were allocated to the newly established business entity.

Following the establishment of the open joint stock company, the TransContainer Department of the Russian Railway Ministry was transformed into a branch of the RZD and further into the subsidiary – the Center for Cargo Container Traffic, TransContainer.

Figure 1. Block diagram of container transport logistics management and routine management of the RZD subsidiary assets

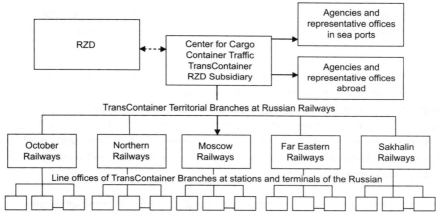

TransContainer formally launched its business on 1 July 2006. A fleet of high-capacity containers and container platforms as well as container terminals/sites (103 terminals in total) at 47 railway stations opened for container operations were contributed to the company's authorized capital.

The company's business results in 2006 were assessed as positive with the net profit of about 1.4 billion rubles. The company owns 23 thousand units of rolling stock and about 50 thousand high capacity containers. A significant portion of the movable property has been renewed and expanded using the income earned by the company, which was in fact one of the objectives of the structural reforms.

TransContainer performs its business operations under contracts signed with legal entities and individuals. In 2006, the company signed over 50 thousand contracts for rendering transportation and forwarding services including the operator services.

In terms of geography and scope of the rendered services, TransContainer claims, and the fact proves it, to be the national containerized cargo transportation operator. Despite the initial problems of the transition period, TransContainer managed to maintain positive development in containerized cargo transportation. For example, in 2006, the total cargo traffic was 21.3 million tons, which was 2.65 million tons more than in 2005. In the same period, the total number of containers transported increased by 3.5 per cent. The loaded-trip-to-empty-trip ratio decreased significantly from about 7 per cent in 2004-2005 to 2 per cent in 2006. The volume of both export and import traffic increased. The share of TransContainer in the transportation market is now 63.4 per cent, which includes transportation by using its own as well as other parties' rolling stocks. These achievements clearly indicate the existence of a growing market and positive results of investments in rolling stocks for containerized cargo transportation.

The three-level management structure developed by the container company ensures optimum combination of strategic and tactical management that are in line with the railway transport management system and provides opportunity for extending and diversifying the range of transport and logistics services. However, an assessment has revealed that a large portion of the company's physical assets, primarily the terminal facilities, requires significant restructuring and upgrading.

The planned level of investment for 2007 is 5 billion rubles, 3 billion of which are borrowed funds. Out of this total investment outlay, 1.7 billion rubles are allocated for the development of a network of branches and agencies and about 150 million rubles alone to be spent for the development of the container terminal in Zabaikalsk. But the major part of the investment is to be used in procuring modern rolling stock. The terminal services will be gradually developed. In particular, appropriate amount of funds will be allocated on an annual basis for procuring modern cargo handling equipment.

TransContainer cooperates with the Moscow State University of Railway Transport in providing targeted training for students in container transportation and logistics. The training programme of the University will be modified to become consistent the requirements of the company's core business.

At present the transportation industry, particularly the containerized cargo transportation sector, exhibits a global trend towards vertical integration. The trend is to create new business configurations through establishment of a new generation of logistics companies that combine the separate stages of goods flow, such as shipment using a combination of various modes of transportation, and storage and distribution into one logistics chain. Worldwide, many transport service providers have implemented this type of new arrangement for container transportation. This trend in greater vertical integration in the industry has been further enhanced through advancement of technological capabilities of the service providers and through the greater use of their own terminal infrastructure and network of agencies along the key routes of freight flow.

The recent positive experience shows the prospects for development of logistics operations by the Russian Railways in containerized cargo transportation. It also indicates the ways to proceeding with the structural reforms for extending the range of transportation and logistics services as well as providing new services by the existing operators. A systems approach allows for modeling complex business processes in both short- and long-term perspectives. Based on the outcome of such modeling exercises, each business process needs to be supported by a specific structural arrangement and appropriate levels of assets together with right pricing policy, which is one of the most important tools to generate business. Redirecting the foreign container flows to RZD is especially important in this context. This goal of redirecting foreign container flows can be achieved through the provision of more attractive condition and the establishment of a network of the company's business representatives, partners and various legal entities of interest abroad.

This approach would allow TransContainer to identify the form and methods of further business development in the area of container transportation primarily by railway and with advanced technological capabilities. It would also allow to considering possible diversification of the company itself. In this respect, joint collaboration with other entities is another example of the company's new business development strategy. For example, ContainerTransScandinavia, a joint venture has been established with the Finnish Railroads to share a portion of the container traffic from Finland to the Russian Federation and vice versa. This joint effort resulted in containerized cargo transportation by the Polar Lights container freight trains running between Helsinki and Moscow.

Thanks to its new strategy for business development, TransContainer has been able to generate new businesses with other countries. The representative office opened by TransContainer in the Republic of Korea allowed the company to sign a contract with LG Electronics for the transportation of component parts for the car manufacturing industry to the Russian Federation. The expected volume of traffic is about 9.6 thousand TEUs per year. A similar representative office is being established in Germany. As a result of this initiative, TransContainer succeeded in signing a lucrative agreement with Germany-based Schenker (a Deutshe Bahn subsidiary) for joint delivery of Volkswagen component parts. TransContainer is also engaged in other international projects. The main routes of currently operating container block trains are shown in table 1.

Table 1. Main routes of container block trains

Main routes of container block trains
Beijing – Moscow
Buslovskaya – Nakhodka – Vostochnaya – Buslovskaya
Berlin – Moscow "Eastwind"
Odessa – Moscow "Odessa"
Budapest – Moscow "Chardesh"
Pravdinsk – Saint Petersburg
Solikamsk – Saint Petersburg
Nigozero – Saint Petersburg
Ust-Ilimsk – Nakhodka – Vostochnaya – Vladivostok
Buslovskaya – Moscow
Nakhodka – Vostochnaya – Brest
Brest – Iletzk
Klaipeda – Moscow
Koity – Saint Petersburg
Saint Petersburg – Sverdlovsk
Moscow – Novosibirsk
Moscow – Krasnoyarsk
Moscow – Irkutsk
Moscow – Khabarovsk
Nakhodka – Moscow
Novosibirsk – Irkutsk
Novosibirsk – Khabarovsk
Saint Petersburg – Khabarovsk
Nakhodka – Vostochnaya – Lokot
Brest – Naushki
Muuga – Moscow

It may be mentioned here that most of these routes are along the famous Trans-Siberian railway which connects Moscow and Saint Petersburg in the west to the Pacific Ocean and port of Vladivostok in the east of the country.

Since delays are anticipated in undertaking structural reforms of the railway transport systems in some of the CIS member countries, the existing arrangements with their railways in the area of container transportation are still maintained through the representative offices and agencies established in those countries. It may be mentioned here that all the representative offices and agencies established abroad directly report to TransContainer. However, for routine operations they report to the Service Center established within TransContainer.

The specialization of container transportation management in the Russian Federation makes it considerably easier to interact on a wide range of issues with foreign business entities of a similar type as well as with international organizations working on large scale projects. In particular, this applies to the close and fruitful cooperation with the United Nations Economic and Social Commission for Asia and the Pacific (ESCAP) on the issues related to arranging demonstration runs of container block trains along the Northern corridor of the Trans-Asian Railway. It is expected that such projects would make a significant contribution to integration of the Russian Federation into international efforts in developing an integrated intermodal international transportation system for the benefit of all participating countries.

CONTAINER TRANSPORTATION BY RAIL: WHICH DIRECTION WILL THAILAND PURSUE?

Chula Sukmanop*

ABSTRACT

The improvement of railway freight services including container transportation is an important element of Thailand's Logistics Development Strategy (2007-2011). For this, the State Railway of Thailand (SRT) is implementing a number of reform measures and physical projects to enhance the capacity and efficiency of the railway freight service. Under a new policy, the Government will take the responsibility for making investments in infrastructure and SRT will remain responsible for network management and administration. In the future, the freight sector will be opened to private operators who would be allowed to invest in their own locomotives and rolling stock and provide services by paying a network access charge to SRT. SRT will be required to compete with private operators.

The article discusses these reform measures and provides an account of the projects that are being implemented or are under consideration to improve SRT's competitiveness and capacity to provide more efficient freight services. It also provides an account of the railway freight transportation in Thailand and its future potential. Finally, it draws conclusions on the on-going reform measures.

AN OVERVIEW ON DEVELOPMENT STRATEGIES OF THAILAND

The Government of Thailand is committed to improving people's standard of living and quality of life. Thailand's Tenth National Economic and Social Development Plan outlines the country's development agenda. The Plan, to be implemented between 2007-2011, aims for balance and sustainability in all areas of development. It focuses on effective utilization of

*   Chula Sukmanop, Senior Expert in Policy and Planning, Head of Multimodal Transport Development Group, Office of the Permanent Secretary, Ministry of Transport, Thailand.

the country's economic, social and natural resources to empower Thai society at all levels and strengthen institutional capacity throughout the country, which would in turn improve Thailand's potential as a knowledge-based society. Priority areas in the Plan include human and social capital development, community strengthening, economic restructuring, environmental diversity, and good governance.

One of the new development strategies for economic restructuring under the 10th Plan is basic infrastructure and logistics development through rail, road and water transport to lower cost and increase competitiveness. The strategy has also been reflected in Thailand's Logistics Development Strategy (2007–2011) where the vision of development is to establish a world-class logistics system to support Thailand as Indochina's trade and investment centre. The objectives are to enhance trade facilitation through improvement of cost efficiency and customer responsiveness of businesses, including reliability and security of their logistics process, and to create economic value from the logistics and other supporting industries. It is expected that logistics cost of the country will reduce from 19 per cent of GDP in 2005 to 16 per cent by 2011. The Strategy has five strategic agenda: Business Logistics Improvement; Transport and Logistics Network Optimization; Logistics Service Internationalization; Trade Facilitation Enhancement; and Capacity Building.

The Ministry of Transport will take the leading role in implementing the second strategic agenda: Transport and Logistics Network Optimization. The target of this agenda is to establish an integrated transport network and logistics management system which will cover the activities of collection and distribution of goods and transhipment at both national and regional levels, and will accommodate and support the role of Thailand to become the trade hub in the Indochina subregion. One of the measures clearly stated under this agenda is to promote transport management for energy saving by giving priority to rail, water and pipeline transport. However, it is important to be noted that this is the first time that there is a clear policy statement specifying that the Government will be responsible for rail infrastructure investment while the role of the State Railway of Thailand (SRT), a public enterprise under the Ministry of Transport, will be restricted to network management, administration and carriage of passengers. In the future, SRT needs to compete with the private sector operators who will be allowed to invest in their own locomotives and rolling stocks for providing carriage of goods services.

I. CHALLENGE IN RAIL TRANSPORT

The efficiency of Thailand's transport system is an important issue. As transport is an essential supporting sector for the whole economy, gains in transport efficiency will lower production and distribution costs and also help improve the country's foreign trade.

Thailand's recent economic growth has led to significant increase in demand for transportation. So far as domestic transport is concerned, road transport has represented about 90 per cent share of the total demand for transportation. In spite of all the advantages of rail transport in terms of fuel efficiency, environmental friendliness, traffic congestion and safety, it remains a relatively minor player in the country compared to road transport. Rail transport accounts for about 15 per cent of all inter-provincial passenger traffic and only 2 per cent of all inter-provincial freight traffic. To a large extent, this is due to a relatively poor competitive position of rail compared to road and other modes transportation. The principal disadvantage of rail transport for freight services is due to its inability to provide door-to-door services. As SRT does not connect directly with the origins or destinations of the main freight flows, the overall transport cost involves trucking at either end of the journey, with high handling costs for transferring from truck to train and vice versa. For short distances, this additional cost is greater than any savings gained by rail transport.

In order to implement the underlining policy to make rail more competitive to road transport and the commitment to adopt measures to switch the mode of transport from road to rail,[1] the current problems faced by railways will be redressed. For example, new rail infrastructure development will be invested by the Government. The debt payments for the previous infrastructure development carried out by SRT will also be borne by the Government. With the government investment, rail tracks will become a common facility like roads, which users can utilize by paying access charges.

At present, the rail service is not a real alternative for the carriage of most goods and passengers, despite its obvious potential benefits in terms of energy efficiency, environmental impacts, and safety. In order to reduce logistics cost to improve the country's competitiveness, and in view of the recent energy crisis, "modal shift from road to rail" has been one of the main

---

[1]   Although the Ministry of Transport intends to develop railways to play a more active role in the nation's future transport needs, road transport retains the importance as it enables door-to-door transportation from the origin to the final destination.

transport policies. In this respect, priority of development has been given to container transportation in the corridor between the main origins and destinations of export and import cargoes and the gateway ports. This would involve deployment of more dedicated container trains, more intermodal facilities at key locations throughout Thailand where containers can be transferred from rail to trucks or ships and vice versa.

II. THE WAY FORWARD TO PROMOTE CONTAINER TRANSPORTATION BY RAIL

A. Demand for rail transport

There has been little change in the structure of imported and exported goods in Thailand in the last five years. In 2004, the volume of freight traffic was about 500 million tons, of which 96 million tons was imported goods and 87 million tons of exported goods, and the rest was domestic. The main import markets of Thailand are Japan (23 per cent), ASEAN (17 per cent), the European Union (10 per cent) and the United States of America (8 per cent), whereas the main export markets are ASEAN (22 per cent), the United States of America (16 per cent), and Japan and the European Union (14 per cent each). The commodity wise structures of imported and exported goods are shown in figure 1.

Figure 1. The structure of imported and exported goods in 2004

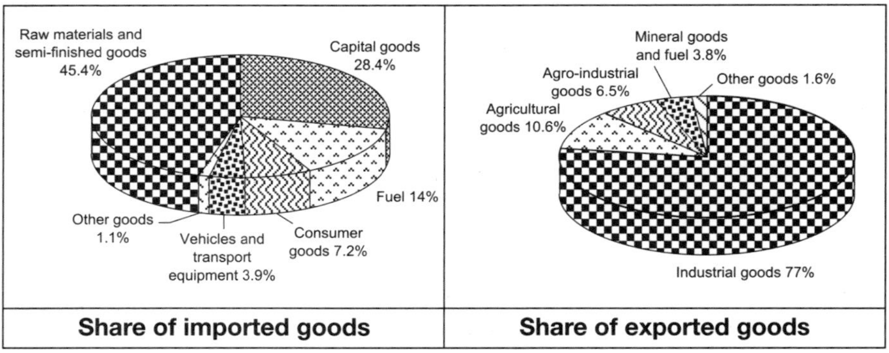

Share of imported goods	Share of exported goods

Source: Study on the Development of Multimodal Transport and Logistics Supply Chain Management for Implementation of Action Plan 2006.

A commodity flow survey was undertaken for the top 20 high value imported goods, the top 12 high value exported goods, the top 10 high net export value goods, and the top 10 of the high volume transit goods.[2] It was found that the selected imported goods had main destinations at Bangkok and its vicinity and industrial estates, especially the eastern industrial estate and the upper-central industrial estate.   For the selected exported goods, the main origins were located at the central, northeast and lower-north regions of Thailand.   The main gateways for the import and export goods were Laem Chabang Port, Bangkok Port, Maptaphut Port, Songkhla Port, Ko Si Chang Port and Bangkok International Airport.

Figure 2 shows the main flows of the selected imported and exported goods.

Figure 2. The flows of selected imported and exported goods

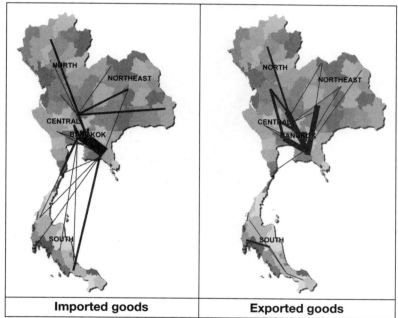

| Imported goods | Exported goods |

Source: Study on the Development of Multimodal Transport and Logistics Supply Chain Management for Implementation of Action Plan 2006, Office of Transport and Traffic Policy and Planning, Ministry of Transport.

---

[2]   The survey is a part of a study on "The Development of Multimodal Transport and Logistics Supply Chain Management for Implementation of Action Plan" made by the Office of Transport and Traffic Policy and Planning in 2006. The 52 commodities included in the survey represent 50 per cent of the overall weight of international freight traffic of Thailand and 18 per cent of the country's total freight traffic.

Thailand provides transit corridor to the Lao People's Democratic Republic for its trade with third countries. In 2004, the volume of export cargo from the Lao People's Democratic Republic transiting Thailand to third countries was 190,000 tons, while the volume of its import cargo from third countries transiting Thailand was 100,000 tons. The main points through which the transit traffic passed were at Nong Khai, Nakhon Phanom, Mukdahan and Phibun Mangsa Han.

Figure 3 shows the main flows of the import, export, transit and domestic goods traffic in 2004. The figure also shows that the transportation activities concentrate in Bangkok and the surrounding areas. The movement of

Figure 3. Flows of the main import, export, transit and domestic goods traffic

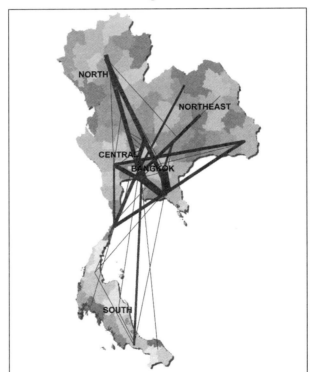

Source: Study on the Development of Multimodal Transport and Logistics Supply Chain Management for Implementation of Action Plan 2006, Office of Transport and Traffic Policy and Planning, Ministry of Transport.

goods was mainly between the north and northeastern areas and the eastern seaboard where Laem Chabang port is located. Coastal shipping had a role in transporting goods from the Southern provinces to Bangkok and Laem Chabang ports.

As the supplier of rail transport, SRT is the sole responsible agency for building, operating and maintaining Thailand's railway infrastructure and providing both passengers and freight carriage services. SRT is the second largest state enterprise of Thailand in terms of manpower. The total length of railroads is about 4,100 km, serving 47 provinces in the country. The main

Figure 4. SRT network

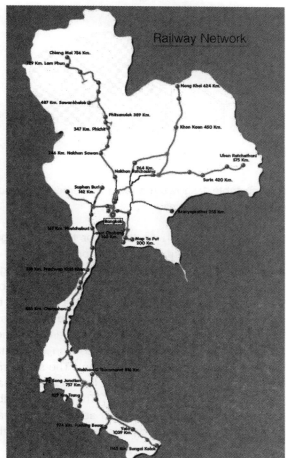

Source: www.railway.co.th.

points of linkage between rail and road transports are Bangkok Port, Laem Chabang Port and ICD Ladkrabang. The railway network can also link with neighbouring countries. It links the Lao People's Democratic Republic via Nong Khai station, Cambodia via Aranyaprathet station, and Malaysia via Padang Besar and Sungai Kolok stations.

In 2004, 12.8 million tons of freight was transported by rail, constituting 7.6 million tons of containerized freight, 3.1 millions tons of fuel and petroleum products and 2.1 million tons of combined cement, stone and sand.

Figure 5. Share of commodity cargo by rail transport, 2004

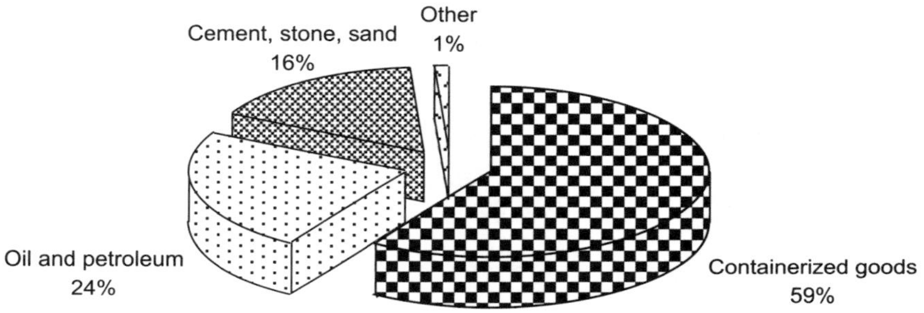

Cement, stone, sand 16%
Other 1%
Oil and petroleum 24%
Containerized goods 59%

Source: State Railway of Thailand.

The following table 1 shows the main movements of goods carried by rail and their origins and destinations.

The information (in table 1) on the major flows of cargoes and their service routes shows the priority areas for promoting rail transport of containerized cargo are between ICD Ladkrabang and Chachoengsao Junction-Sri Racha Junction-Laem Chabang Port. The container traffic moving over this section has grown rapidly over the years. It can also be seen that there has been a high demand of rail transport between the northeastern (Nakhon Ratchasima Province) and central (Saraburi Province) areas of the country and Laem Chabang Port where some export cargoes can be containerized and transferred to the port via Chachoengsao Junction. The southern corridor has also high potential as it provides the railway link between Thailand and its southern neighbours Malaysia and Singapore. The current landbridge service between Malaysia and Thailand, a rail container service for the transhipment of containers between ICDs in Thailand and ports in Malaysia, uses this corridor.[3]

---

[3]   A companion article in this volume is on this landbridge service.

Table 1. Major flows of cargoes by rail, 2004

Commodity	Routes		Volume (tons)
	From	To	
Containerized cargo	ICD Ladkrabang	Laem Chabang Port	3 861 400
	Laem Chabang Port	ICD Ladkrabang	2 929 516
	ICD Ladkrabang	Tha Rua Noi (Kanchanaburi)	143 439
	Nuon Payom (Kohn Khen)	Laem Chabang Port	116 422
	ICD Ladkrabang	Phahonyothin	91 445
	Tha Rua Noi (Kanchanaburi)	ICD Ladkrabang	77 809
	Surat Thani	ICD Ladkrabang	45 500
	Jira Junction (Nakorn Ratchasima)	ICD Ladkrabang	45 054
	Surat Thani	Bangkok Port	39 948
	Huey Gueng (Udon Thani)	Laem Chabang Port	38 720
Fuel and petroleum product	Bung Phra (Phitsanulok)	Laem Chabang Port	573 187
	Bung Phra (Phitsanulok)	Bangkok Port	571 080
	Map Ta Phut	Khon Kaen	254 599
	Map Ta Phut	Lam Pang	190 907
Cement	Hin Lap (Nakhon Ratchasima)	Preng (Chachoengsao)	375 951
	Hin Lap (Nakhon Ratchasima)	Phahonyothin	320 779
	Ban Chong Tai (Saraburi)	Phahonyothin	319 722
Stone	Bu Yai (Saraburi)	Ladkrabang	367 049
Gypsum	Ban Song (Surat Thani)	Padang Besar	95 308
Flour	Phahonyothin	Padang Besar	16 543
Rubber	Thungsong Junction	Bangkok Post	18 068
Noodle	Ban Pong (Ratchaburi)	Padang Besar	4 352
Sugar	Buriram	Laem Chabang Port	2 271

Source: State Railway of Thailand.

B. Policies, strategies, and plans/projects intended to improve the capacity and efficiency of the rail services

Improvement of essential infrastructure and related facilities

Inadequate railway infrastructure and facilities cause disruptive train operations. The improvement of rail infrastructure and facilities that are currently being considered can be divided into five categories: double tracking, track rehabilitation, construction of chord lines, new network expansion, and upgrading of signalling and telecommunication systems.

Measures for substantial improvement of rail tracks will be undertaken. In the sections where the traffic volume is high and there is high potential for new users of rail services, double tracking will be considered. This will greatly increase capacity by providing a separate railway line for each direction of travel rather than having to share a single line for two way movements. An initial study carried out by SRT shows that about 800 km of double tracks are needed to facilitate freight transportation by rail.

It has been agreed that the first priority double tracking will be in the Eastern Seaboard Area. The 78 km double tracking project to be started in 2007 will connect Chachoengsao Junction to Laem Chabang Port. The other double tracking project in the pipeline is 106 km section between Chachoengsao-Klong Sib Kao-Kaeng Khoi and further towards Nakhon Ratchasima. This project will serve the demand of traffic between the north-eastern provinces and the Eastern Seaboard.

Figure 6. Double Tracking Project between Chachoengsao, Klong Sib Kao and Khaeng Khoi Junctions

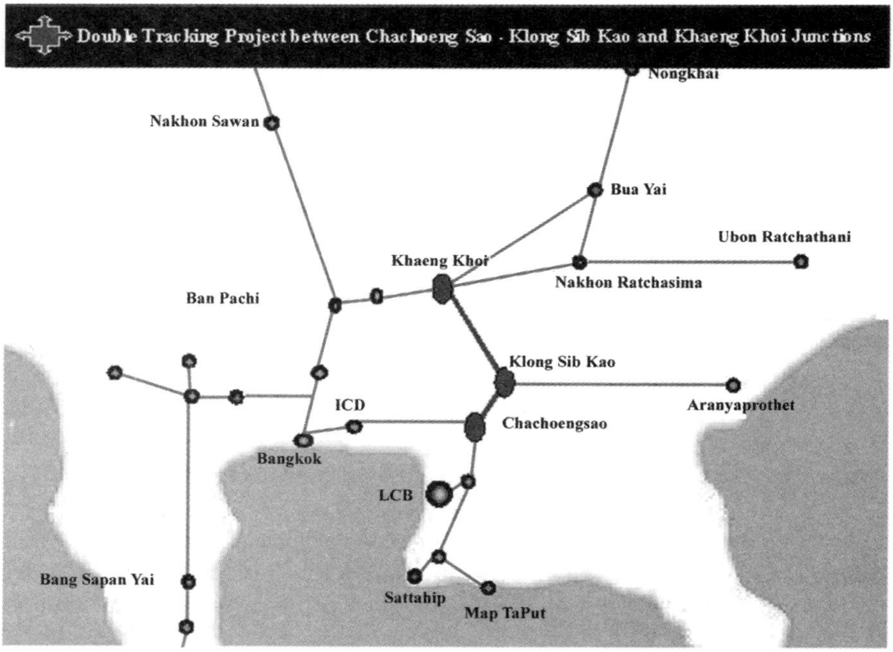

The other routes that require special attention for double tracking are about 150 km of the northern line between Lopburi and Nakhon Sawan, and 336 km of the Southern Line between Nakhon Pathom-Petchburi-Chumphon-Surat Thani-Nakhon Sri Thammarat.

Track rehabilitation involves replacing existing rails with heavier rail sections and concrete sleepers. This permits higher train speeds and lower maintenance costs. A recent study by SRT also shows that about 810 km of track rehabilitation covering many areas of the north, north-eastern and southern lines are needed for the improvement of speed and punctuality of train operation and avoidance of derailment. Such rehabilitation incorporates the replacement of existing 70 lb rails with 100 lb rails, the replacement of existing sleepers with monoblock concrete sleepers together with elastic rail fastenings and reballasting and improvement of embankment.

Apart from increasing the track capacity, construction of few chord lines is also being considered to reduce the distance between some major nodes on the rail network. An initial study by SRT shows that three such chord lines are needed. These are as mentioned below:

- A 1-km chord line at Chachoengsao junction to connect the eastern line (Aranyaprathet line) and the eastern seaboard line (Sattahip line);

- A 3.4-km chord line at Khang Khoi junction to connect the north-eastern line and the eastern line (Kaeng Khoi–Klong Sip Kao);

- A 1-km chord line at Ban Phachi junction to connect the northern line and the north-eastern line.

The expansion of the network to recently established transport terminals or new gateways are being planned. It has been suggested that an extension of approximately 320 km of the northern line from Denchai to the Mekong river port at Chieng San or Chieng Kong (where there is a bridge across the Mekong River) be constructed so that goods from Southern China can be carried by road via the Lao People's Democratic Republic and transferred to rail for further transport towards the sea ports in Thailand. Moreover, an extension of the north-eastern line from Bua Yai to Roi Et-Mukdahan-Nakhon Panom, over a length of approximately 368 km, will also help the linkage between Thailand and the Lao People's Democratic Republic and Viet Nam. However, implementation of the above projects will require huge investments. It is expected that the feasibility studies on the proposed railway extensions will be reviewed and updated before resubmitting them to the Government for approval.

Signalling and telecommunications upgrading will provide more efficient control of railway operations and achieve significant time savings by eliminating or reducing train delays. Subsequently, when the existing rolling

Figure 7. Chord Line Projects at Chachoengsao, Kaeng Khoi and Ban Pachi Junctions

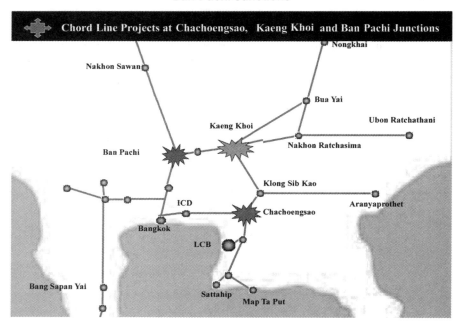

stock needs to be replaced, they will be replaced by modern rolling stocks which will allow higher speed. The signalling and telecommunications upgrading programme will be implemented in conjunction with the double tracking project mentioned earlier.[4]

Improvement of operation and management system and restructuring of rail transport service

During the period when the infrastructure development and modernization of operation facilities are taking place, the freight transport services provided by SRT needs to be improved in terms of reliability, journey time, service and customer satisfaction to increase its share of the freight transport market, particularly through modal shift from other modes. It is also expected that, to improve the services, SRT must be prepared to consider other measures, which include new locomotives and rolling stock, development of inland container depots and container yards, change in the existing service

---

[4]   For more details on SRT's infrastructure development and signalling and telecommunications upgrading projects, see www.railway.co.th/english/index.asp.

operation, forging strategic partnerships, and new marketing initiatives and other necessary measures.

At the moment, the Ministry of Transport is preparing to open the rail transport market to private operators. The private service operators are to pay access charges to SRT for using its infrastructure. The private operators will provide services with their own locomotives and wagons. While acting as a rail operator, SRT will have to compete with private franchisees on the common rail network. It is expected that SRT will issue regulations specifying the procedures on the matter within 2007. After the establishment of a Rail Regulator and the amendments of the necessary legislations, any interested private party may apply for rail operation directly from the regulator.

It may also be noted that the Government is now in the process of reforming the structure of rail transport service. Due to its past financial condition, SRT was not in a position to make any heavy investments to improve services or build infrastructure to meet the transport demand in the future. Since rail transport will have direct impacts on future competitiveness of the country and the Government has recognized SRT's problem as a national problem, the responsibility of rail transport development between the government and SRT has been reallocated. Under the new rail transport management structure approved by the cabinet in July 2007, the Government will provide annual budget allocations for network development similar to what have been done for the road transport. The role of SRT will be restricted to infrastructure maintenance and operation and as a rail transport operator. A safety and economic regulator for rail transport will be established. Also, a clear line will be drawn between social rail service and commercial rail service. There will be a detailed settlement arrangement for the subsidy that the Government will give to SRT for the provision of public service obligation (PSO) services and for infrastructure maintenance and operation. For this purpose, there will be a separate capital account for social rail service of the government to handle the costs of social service. Under this arrangement SRT will act as a hired service provider.

According to the Action Plan for the Improvement of Management Structure for the Revival of Financial Status of the State Railway of Thailand, which will be submitted to the cabinet for approval, the structure of SRT will be reorganized in four business units. These four units are: Infrastructure and Traffic Control; Freight Transport; Passenger Transport; and General Service. Three new subsidiary companies will also be established: Eastern Line Freight Transport Management Company Limited, Electric and Commuter Train Management Company Limited and SRT Asset Management Company Limited.

The Plan also covers strategies to strengthen SRT's financial condition. The Government has been requested to compensate 2.2 billion baht liability from the loss in running business and 1.4 billion baht liability for infrastructure investment made by SRT. In return, SRT will be required to transfer SRT's land currently utilized by government agencies worth about 4 billion baht to the Treasury Department. The improvement of the pension scheme is also a part of the reform package.

CONCLUSION

Despite its commonly-accepted benefits in terms of energy efficiency, environmental impacts and safety, rail transport has rarely been taken into consideration by users of the freight transportation service. The Ministry of Transport has for the last five years made attempts to promote a modal shift from road to rail with special attention being paid to certain commodities and between certain origins to destinations. Intermodal transport with rail transport performing the main carriage has been promoted as an alternative to a single mode of road transport. Import and export of containerized cargoes such as rice, sugar and manioc products are the main target groups of the future rail transport users.

The Government has a firm policy that the future rail network development will come from the annual budget and there will be a joint responsibility between the government and SRT in infrastructure maintenance and operation. The Ministry of Transport is formulating plans to progressively improve the efficiency of export and import container transportation via Laem Chabang Port. At the moment, Ladkrabang ICD is the main node for mode transfer from road to rail. The priority of development is therefore the removal of bottleneck between this node and the port. The remaining 78 km double tracking of the corridor will begin this year and is expected to be completed by 2009. The double tracking project will continue further towards Nakhon Ratchasima and Nakhon Sawan from where there are high potential demands for rail transport. With such initial infrastructure improvement, the nodes for rail transfer to/from the port will be moved nearer to the final origins/destinations of export/import traffic. The route will also give benefit to domestic cross-country bulk cargo movement. The role of rail transportation will then be more significant to exporters, importers and domestic users.

In concurrence with infrastructure improvement, the market of freight transport services will be gradually opened to private operators. Private operators will be allowed to provide services under a franchising agreement with SRT.

The improvement of rail transport cannot be completed without the reform of SRT. The reform is intended to improve financial condition of SRT and enable it to provide services efficiently to meet the future freight transportation demand and to become competitive with other private operators. The new structure will allow SRT to separate capital account in accordance with the activities and will be an effective tool for implementing the overall policy for rail transport development. A newly-established subsidiary company will focus on container transportation between Ladkrabang ICD and Laem Chabang Port.

Thailand wants to improve the efficiency and reliability of rail transport services. The assumption of responsibility of railway network improvement by government, the reform of SRT's role and organizational structure with new subsidy schemes and the private participation in rail transport market are among the main directions that Thailand will pursue in the future. It is hoped that improvement of container transportation by rail will lay an important foundation for the country's intermodal transport system and enhance its capacity to serve neighboring countries as the transit corridor to or from third countries.

THE DEVELOPMENT OF CONTAINER LANDBRIDGE TRAIN SERVICES BETWEEN MALAYSIA AND THAILAND

A. Valautham*

BACKGROUND

Containerization in Malaysia began in 1973 when the first container vessel berthed at Port Klang. Although containers had gone through Port Klang much earlier, those came by conventional vessels and were unloaded by using the ship's own gear as the quayside equipment for container handling was not available at that time. In order to serve the growing need of container movement, container handling facilities were introduced at major ports of Port Klang, Penang, Kota Kinabalu, Sandakan, Sibu and Kuching.

Subsequent to this development in the port sector, and as a preparation to overland container transportation by railways, in 1972 the then Malayan Railway successfully ran a special train of mock up containers made of wooden structure to determine the clearance on all bridges and in tunnels. After the successful trial run and making necessary facilities available, container transportation by railways in Malaysia started in 1974. From an initial carriage of 974 TEU in 1974, container transportation by railways in the country has grown over the years to more than 334,300 TEU by the end of 2006 (see figure 1).

I. CROSS BORDER TRAFFIC

Container haulage by rail: KTMB container and landbridge services

The container haulage operation by railways is carried out by Keretapi Tanah Melayu Berhad (KTMB), the Malaysian State Railway Authority. Apart from container haulage from Port Klang, Penang and until recently from the Port of Tanjung Pelepas, KTMB's rail connection also links to Inland Clearance Depots (ICDs) at Ipoh Cargo Terminal, Sg Way, Nilai Inland Port and Segamat Inland Port.

---

*   Senior Manager, Strategic Business Unit, Keretapi Tanah Melayu Berhad Corporate Headquarters, Kuala Lumpur; e-mail: valautham@ktmb.com.my.

Figure 1. Container carried by rail from 1974-2006 (TEUs)

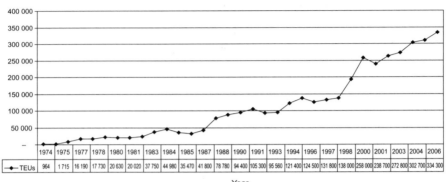

	1974	1975	1977	1978	1980	1981	1983	1984	1985	1987	1988	1990	1991	1993	1994	1996	1997	1998	2000	2001	2003	2004	2006
TEUs	964	1 715	16 190	17 730	20 630	20 020	37 750	44 980	35 470	41 800	78 780	94 400	105 300	95 560	121 400	124 500	131 800	138 000	258 000	238 700	272 800	302 700	334 300

Year

KTMB also operates a landbridge service in collaboration with the State Railway of Thailand (SRT). The landbridge service permits cross border movement of containers between Malaysia and Thailand by railways. The service links the Malaysian ports having railheads with the ICDs at Bang Sue and Lat Krabang in Thailand. The service is currently managed by four private operators, namely T.S. Transrail (M) Sdn Bhd, Freight Management (M) Sdn Bhd, T.S. Allied Solution Sdn Bhd and PTP Landbridge Services Sdn Bhd. It provides a third alternative to road and sea transports between Malaysia and Thailand, as well as an overland transit linkage from the Malaysian ports to third countries in the ASEAN subregion namely, Cambodia, the Lao People's Democratic Republic and Viet Nam.

Container haulage by railways was developed as one of the means to reduce congestion and improve efficiency of the ports. In 2006, KTMB carried more than 334,000 TEU, which represented an annual average growth rate of about 8.6 per cent between 1999 and 2006. In order to provide a door-to-door service and improve the quality of service, KTMB has introduced the concept of intermodal transport in its container haulage operation. It has formed a subsidiary road haulage company called Multimodal Freight Sdn Bhd to facilitate its intermodal haulage operation. In order to enhance the capacity of container haulage by rail, the Government has allocated M$ 4.5 billion in the Eighth Malaysia Plan for double tracking of the main railway line that will eventually connect Padang Besar at the Malaysia-Thailand border with Johor Bahru at the Malaysia-Singapore border. Apart from this, the Government is also contemplating a railway link connecting the city of Kunming in China with Singapore via Malaysia, which would further boost the role of railways in container transportation in the region.

A Joint Traffic Agreement between the State Railway of Thailand and the Malayan Railway was made in 1954 to facilitate the free flow of goods between the two neighbouring countries.[1] Currently, the Joint Traffic Agreement is being reviewed and a draft has been submitted to Governments of both the countries for their approval.

A variety of goods are transported across the border of Malaysia and Thailand. Goods that mainly constitute the current cross border traffic include cement, gypsum, food products and containerized cargo. The main flows of goods between the points in two countries take place as follows:

(a)   Cement from Bukit Ketri (Malaysia) to Wakaf Bharu (Malaysia) to Thailand via Hatyai;

(b)   Gypsum from Thong Soon (Thailand) to various cement plants in Malaysia;

(c)   Food products from Bangkok, Thailand to Malaysia;

(d)   Containers between ICDs in Thailand and ports and ICDs in Malaysia.

The transportation of cement between the two countries was not covered under the 1954 Agreement. To permit cement transportation, an addendum was made to the Joint Traffic Agreement in 1989 which was signed by the Ministers of Transport of the two countries.

The cross border trade and traffic received a big boost when the landbridge container train services from Sri Setia in Malaysia to Bangsue, Thailand were launched in 1999. The landbridge train services also marked a new era in the rail transportation industry in the ASEAN subregion.

II. THE GENERAL CONCEPT OF LANDBRIDGE

The landbridge concept was first conceived in the early 1960s to promote a more efficient means of shipping between East Asia and Europe. It is an intermodal service involving land and sea transport as an alternative to transportation service entirely by sea. Many landbridge services are now operated in the world. Some well-known landbridge operations in different parts of world are mentioned below.

---

[1]   The cross-border agreement between the two railways was originally made in 1922. This agreement was amended in 1954 to incorporate upgrades in technical standards of railways.

Table 1. Freight traffic between Malaysia and Thailand (tons)

	1990	1997	1998	1999	2000	2001	2002	2003	2004	2005	2006
Inbound	409 845	355 720	285 677	123 961	112 390	103 195	110 343	86 920	40 724	59 153	20 975
Outbound	31 804	35 338	39 264	43 627	48 473	53 859	64 469	66 243	74 885	78 391	86 211
Landbridge Traffic	–	–	–	75 948	281 520	164 704	169 132	200 874	215 982	152 504	152 135
Total	441 649	391 058	324 941	243 536	442 383	321 758	343 944	354 037	331 591	290 048	259 321

Note: The landbridge service started in June 1999.

The North-American landbridge links the two major gateway systems of North America. It links the major ports on the west coast (Los Angeles and Long Beach) and New York/New Jersey on the east coast via Chicago. The landbridge also has a Canadian and a Mexican section. The landbridge service offers an alternative to freight shipment between Asia and the American east coast via the Panama Canal or the Straight of Magellan. By operating double-stack container trains between the east and west coasts of the United States of America the landbridge service offers a significant reduction in shipment cost and time between Pacific-Asia and the American east coast. The reduction in shipment time can be from 6 days to two weeks. The landbridge service also competes for a market share of the freight traffic between Asia and West Europe. A significant share of the domestic rail freight in North America is also carried by this service. An important characteristic of this landbridge service is that it provides transcontinental link through a single country namely, Canada, United States or Mexico.

The Mexican Landbridge spans across the Isthmus of Tehuantepec in Mexico.[2] It represents the shortest overland distance of 182 miles between the Gulf of Mexico and the Pacific Ocean linking the Port of Salina Cruz (on the Pacific) and Port of Coatzacoalcos (on the Gulf of Mexico). The overland transport service is provided both by railway and highway carriers. The alternative to this landbridge service is using a sea route via the Panama Canal, which may require ships to wait as long as five days owing to congestion. The landbridge was opened to traffic in 1907. However, it gained prominence in the recent years as an alternative to an all-sea route between East Asia and the American east coast.

---

[2]   An isthmus is a narrow strip of land that is bordered on two sides by water and connects two larger land masses.

The Siberian Landbridge operation is a combination of land and marine transportation between Japan and the Republic of Korea, and Europe and the Central Asia via ports in the Russian far east using the Trans Siberian Railroad. This landbridge service was developed as an alternative to all-marine transportation between North and East Asia and Europe.

III. THE MALAYSIA-THAILAND LANDBRIDGE

Keretapi Tanah Maleyu Berhad (KTMB) and the State Railway of Thailand (SRT) were interested in transporting a part of the large number of maritime containers by rail from Port Klang and Klang Valley to Bangkok and vice versa. The idea conceptualised by the Railways required direct involvement of, and coordination with their counterparts in port authorities and ICDs at Port Klang and Bangkok. The concerned parties realized that a scheduled container block train service between Port Klang and Bangkok would offer a comparative advantage over the sea-route transhipment service of containers to/from Thailand via Singapore or Port Klang. With this business prospect in mind the Malaysia-Thailand Landbridge was launched in 1999. It uses KTMB services for the Malaysian part and the State Railway of Thailand (SRT) services for the Thai part of the journey.

The landbridge service offers intermodal transportation between the Klang Container Terminal, Port Klang or Kontena Nasional Inland Clearance Depot at Seri Setia in Malaysia to Bangsue and Lat Krabang in Thailand. In addition to transhipment service, it facilitates direct export and import of goods from Klang Valley to Bangkok and vice versa. The landbridge service also offers transhipment of containers for a third country by transporting the containers from a Malaysian port.

IV. WHY KTMB DEVELOPED THE LANDBRIDGE SERVICES

There are several factors that led to the development of the landbridge service. As a result of the 1997 Asian financial crisis, ASEAN countries went through a period of recession compounded by the weakening of their currencies against the United States dollar. KTMB suffered a sharp drop in its freight revenue. This decline in revenues required the company to develop a new demand-responsive business strategy for its freight operations with greater emphasis on containerized freight shipment.

Trade tariff rates were being continuously reduced in line with the ASEAN Free Trade Area (AFTA) framework to promote increased volume of inter-country trade in the subregion. This required increased cross-border transportation of goods. As a part of its new strategy, KTMB wanted to position itself as one of the main logistic players and to benefit from the business opportunity provided by the growing trade in the subregion. It was also realized by both the railways that the proposed landbridge service would be a low risk venture for them as it would require minimum additional investment for infrastructure improvement and procurement of necessary equipment. Most of the infrastructural facilities including facilities at border points were already in existence to facilitate scheduled passenger services across the border.

With the advent of the landbridge Services in the year 1999, KTMB was able to increase its overall freight revenues after experiencing declines over the previous three years. As a result of the 1997 financial crisis KTMB was able to capitalize on transportation that was more economical and was able to offer an alternative far more efficient mode of transportation to shippers.

V. BENEFITS OF MOVING GOODS THROUGH RAIL LANDBRIDGE SERVICES

Service features

The landbridge service operators are offering weekly fixed day services between Malaysia and Thailand. The service accepts both import and export cargoes between Malaysia and Thailand and another country in full container load (FCL) of 20 ft and 40 ft sizes including high cubes in both sizes, as well as less than container load (LCL) of the same sizes of containers. The service include terminal-to-terminal, door-to-door, terminal-to-door, or door-to-terminal deliveries of shipment. The freight in FCL mode includes steel, rice, petrochemical products, manufactured goods and electronic parts and freight in LCL mode includes spare parts, food stuff, electrical goods and general merchandise.

Simple documentation procedure

Through the support of Malaysian and Thai Customs formalities can be performed at the port of loading and port of discharge. Goods are cleared at the border station of Padang Besar with minumum clearance formalities that requires only about three hours. The same station building houses custom officials of both the countries. The customs officials only check the documents without physical examination of the cargo contents.

An advantage of container transportation by the landbridge service is that they do no require unloading and reloading for inspection by the customs officials. It may be mentioned here that containers transported by trucks are unloaded and reloaded at a container depot beside the railway yard as it is not allowed to drive trucks into other countries.

Competitive pricing

This service with a shorter transit time and competitive price compared with other modes of transport (for example, about 15 to 30 per cent cheaper than transportation by road) offers a viable alternative to shippers. Landbridge operators offer differential pricing package to suit customers' requirement. An inherent advantage of the railways over road is that railways can carry goods in larger volumes and weight over a longer distance that allows lower cost of transportation per unit. The savings incurred can be passed on to customers in the form of cheaper tariff.

Security features

The containers are sealed as per normal shipping procedures. The Malaysian and Thai Customs will seal the boxes at the port of loading and at the border crossing at Padang Besar. An added security feature of the specialized chassis is provided by KTMB. Because of this safety feature, the doors of the loaded wagons sitting on the chassis cannot be opened fully to discharge the cargo. This feature minimizes any form of pilferage.

A comparison of the container shipment services provided by alternative modes of transportation is provided in table 2.

Table 2. Comparison of transport modes

	Transit time (days)	Freight charge	LCL services	Security	Door-door delivery	Suitability for heavy cargo
Landbridge	3	xx	Yes	xxx	Yes	Good
Air Freight	1	xxxxxx	Yes	xxx	No	Poor
Sea Freight	6	xxx	Yes	xxx	No	Good
Road Transport	3	xxx	Yes	xx	Yes	Fair

Notes: "x" represents average values on Bangkok-Kuala Lumpur route. The interpretation is as follows:

Freight charge: less "x"s means lower cost.
Freight security: more "x"s means lower level of security protection.
LCL : Less than Container Load.

VI. OPERATIONS OF LANDBRIDGE SERVICES

Technical arrangements

The technical aspects of train operations focus on six major areas as follows:

- Infrastructural requirement;

- Rolling stock requirement;

- Motive power requirement;

- Container handling facilities;

- Vessel concept; and

- Transit time.

Infrastructural requirement

The Infrastructural requirements as provided in the Joint Traffic Agreement made by the railways ensure the smooth carriage of containers on both the railways.

Rolling stock requirement

It was agreed that in the initial period years of operation KTMB would provide container wagons which would run everyday with a turnaround time of about five days. It was estimated that minimum of 90 container wagons were required for 6 trips per week for a round-the-clock operation without considering any spare capacity. KTMB agreed to source the Bogie Container Flat Wagons for this new service. The increase in demand for the landbridge services requires more wagons which are currently being supplied only by KTMB. In the future, The State Railway of Thailand (SRT) will have to provide more wagons in order to sustain the growth of landbridge services.

The container wagons can either be of a multipurpose type or dedicated type of custom-built flat wagons. The advantage with multipurpose wagons is that the tare weight can be kept to a minimum. It is essential that all wagons should have a secured locking mechanism to hold the boxes in place. In cases where the overhead structures of the railway system restrict the loading of overheight containers, one possible solution would be to use of wagons fitted with smaller wheels. KTMB has over 200 such low-floor wagons with wheel diameter of 788 mm. Wagons of axle load of at least 15 tons are needed and currently the new fleet of KTMB wagons meets this requirement.

Motive power requirement

For a five-day turnaround time two locomotives are required to have a trailing load of 1,200 tons daily on the Malaysian side.

Container handling facilities

On the Malaysian side, support is provided through container handling facilities at Port Klang and Kontena Nasional Berhad ICD at Seri Setia. The Klang Port Authority and Kontena Nasional Berhad have been supportive and are actively promoting the services, as they also benefit from the landbridge service. Padang Besar remains the transit border township with institutional arrangements made with the support of the Customs Departments of both Malaysia and Thailand.

Vessel concept

It was agreed that the train would be run under the vessel operating concept where the trains would be named and a number would be given to each train, for example, Trans Perdana Voyage No. 007. This voyage concept is contrary to the traditional train operation concept, which was practiced earlier.

Landbridge trains are, run on a full train load concept where possible. It may be mentioned here that KTMB runs most of its container trains on this modality. The container trains in Malaysia run from the ports to the inland areas for one particular customer. The customer undertakes marketing for traffic and organizes the containers available to be run as a complete train or block train. The train is run between two fixed points (one point in each country) as one complete train. The benefits of running a block train include lower operational costs, savings in transit time, and lower the turnaround time of wagons, and locomotives.

The smooth movement of freight trains can guarantee delivery time promised by the service operators to the shippers. To be more precise, the reliability in delivery times, and fewer stops mean decreased risk of accidents, less paperwork, higher productivity, and efficiency and lower cost.

Transit time

Table 3. Distance and transit time by the landbridge service

Distance		
Klang Container Terminal to Padang Besar	Padang Besar to Bangkok	Total distance of train journey
600 km	990 km	1 590 km
Transit time			

Klang Container Terminal to Padang Besar	Border check	Padang Besar to Bangkok	Total transit time
21 hours	3 hours	36 hours	60 hours

As can be seen from the above table that the important selling point in the promotion of the landbridge services to its customers is the reduced transit time of 60 hours, which is significantly lower compared to vessel movement that requires five days. The service is run somewhat similar to the international passenger express train now operating between Bangkok and Kuala Lumpur on a 24-hour journey time.

VII. COMMERCIAL ARRANGEMENTS OF THE LANDBRIDGE SERVICE

The commercial arrangements of the service include the following:

(a)   Landbridge service provider;

(b)   Linkages to other modes of transport;

(c)   Customs documentation and clearance procedures; and

(d)   Container and merchandise liability.

Landbridge service provider

The landbridge service can be provided by the freight forwarders as the non-vessel operating common carrier (NVOCC). They issue the bill of lading for the carriage of goods on trains which they neither own nor operate. The freight forwarders stand to gain significantly from the landbridge operation. This is so because the entire consignment is entrusted under their custody and they become the sole liaison with other components in the whole chain of the transport system.

Currently four operators are involved in providing the service. They are: Freight Management, Profreight Group, T.S. Transrail and Infinity Logistics. The operators base their services on the platform of the two railways of Malaysia and Thailand. As such, some of the physical characteristics of the service are similar. However, there are differences in terms of pricing, container type, quality of terminal services, availability of special equipment, and application of information and communication technology and other value added services. Being attracted by the competitiveness of the landbridge service, some shipping lines are now using the service.

The Port Klang-based freight forwarder Freight Management of Malaysia and Bangkok-based Profreight Group of Thailand jointly operate the Asean Rail Express (ARX). The service is run between Klang, Ipoh and Penang in Malaysia and the Lat Krabang Terminal in Bangkok, Thailand. Currently, ARX is offering 4 weekly fixed day services each way between Malaysia and Thailand. ARX provides terminal-to-terminal, door-to-door, terminal-to-door and door-to-terminal services to suit the need of customers. It also accepts LCL cargo for transhipment through Port Klang to other countries. The ARX service represents a saving of approximately three days in terms of transit time and a saving of up to 10 per cent of shipping costs compared to transhipment via Singapore by sea.

T.S. Transrail's (better known as T.S.) landbridge service connects Kontena Nasional's Inland Clearance Depots (ICDs) at Sungai Way in Setia Jaya, Prai in Penang and the Ipoh Cargo Terminal with Bangsue ICD in Bangkok, Thailand. Shippers receive door-to-door deliveries. Although the service is half a day slower than by road, the rates are about 30 per cent cheaper. T.S. provides 1-2 weekly services.

Infinity Logistics operates services between Malaysia and places in the south of Thailand. Their link points are Klang, Ipoh and Penang in Malaysia and Hatyai/Surat Thani in Thailand. They provide about 1-2 weekly services.

Linkages to other modes of transport

Railways cannot perform landbridge services effectively if they are not directly linked to the seaports, airports, Inland Clearance Depots (ICDs) or Container Yards (CYs). These are the interfacing points where the transfer from one mode to another mode takes place. In order for the railways to capture the container traffic, these linkages are essential.

In Malaysia, the crucial linkages to the ports are clearly recognized and the existing sea ports/facilities are in the process of being rail linked. While planning rail linkages to ports, ICDs and container yards, it is essential that operation and commercial practices be considered from the outset. Otherwise, physical systems may be in place that would increase the operational costs to the railways, as they may not have been designed to meet the particular needs of railways operational and commercial practices.

Customs documentation and clearance procedure

The Malaysian Customs Department has agreed that the present system could be further extended to transhipment of containers provided the landbridge service operators and the shipping lines concerned lodge a *"transit manifest"* covering containers to be moved to the border. Such movements are allowed under bond covered by a Custom 8 (K8) Form. Procedures already exist for sealing and dispatch of containers covered under the arrangements of the K8 Form from KCT to Penang.

Currently, for container movements across the border, the importer appoints a forwarding agent at Padang Besar who then lodges the appropriate documents with the customs authority. However, such lodging process is relevant only to border clearance purpose. Ultimate clearance by the customs is done only at the final destination in Thailand after payment of due duty.

The procedure used for the movement of containers under bond are as follows:

(a)   The Customs seals the containers themselves at KN ICD before endorsing the K8 Form;

(b)   The sealing and endorsement of the K8 Form must be completed before the loading of containers onto rail wagons; and

(c)   Customs at the destination checks containers' numbers and their seals against the original K8 Form carried by the train and included in the manifest of the train.

At the border both Customs jointly inspect container numbers and seals with details appearing in the K8 Forms that are included in the manifest of the train.

If all relevant details are in order, the K8/K2 Form will be endorsed with Customs of both the countries retaining copies while the train proceeds to its final destination. Copies of the endorsed K8/K2 Form must then be sent to the destination points for clearance purposes.

At the destination (Bangsue or Seri Setia), containers will be inspected by the Customs to ensure that container seals and numbers match with details appearing on the K8/K2 Forms.

Liability

With intermodalism making tremendous inroads in the freight transport industry, KTMB had reacted positively by revising its liabilities governing the carriage of containers and its contents to be on par with international maritime container carriage practice. The new liabilities came into force on 1989 and covers Malaysia, Singapore and Thailand.

Insurance

To further enhance confidence, especially for transportation of containers on across border basis, KTMB has had in force, insurance coverage requirements for freight. Box 1 gives some of its important features.

Box 1. Insurance coverage of freight

Insured value: Maximum M$ 5 million per accident.

Territorial limits: Anywhere in West Malaysia including Singapore and Thailand.

Subject matter insured: General Goods/Merchandise of every description belonging to the insured or on commission or for which insurer is responsible whilst in transit by container or non-container including damage to these items while using the railway on Railway track including handling/loading and temporary storage during transit not exceeding 14 days.

(continued to page 112)

(continued from page 111)

The insurance coverage of freight include:

- All additional costs and expenses necessary and reasonably incurred by the insured consequent upon any claim payable or incurred solely to avoid or minimize claim including cost and expenses in the removal and disposal of damaged goods and debris.

- Loss due to destruction of or damage to clothing and personal effects of drivers or other attendants.

- Strike, riot and civil commotion and malicious damage.

- Cross liabilities.

Limits of liability:

- Any one consignment M$ 2.5 million per containerized/non-containerized unit.

  Any one location (temporary storage in course of transit not exceeding 14 days).

Note: The ARX service international liability insurance coverage.

VIII. KEY SUCCESS FACTORS

The key factors for the successful launching of the first landbridge train are:

Sufficient rolling stock

Readily available Malaysian bogie container flats were use for the landbridge operation from Kuala Lumpur to Bangkok.

Sufficient market demand

Unlike the previous attempt to launch a landbridge operation 10 years ago with RCL, there is a huge demand for the service this time around.

Cooperation from customs

Minimum customs inspection at the border allows minimum train detaining time at the border. The cross-border customs clearance process is very smooth.

Cooperation from the private sector

The cooperation between freight forwarders from both countries plays a key role in the success of landbridge services.

Joint Traffic Agreement

Without doubt the most significant contributing factor to the success of the landbridge service is the Joint Traffic Agreement which facilitates the smooth and free running of train operations between both countries.

Figure 2. Landbridge TEU, June 1999 to December 2006

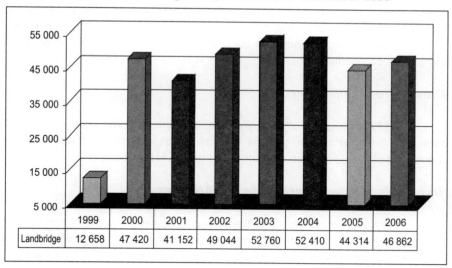

	1999	2000	2001	2002	2003	2004	2005	2006
Landbridge	12 658	47 420	41 152	49 044	52 760	52 410	44 314	46 862

IX. POTENTIAL AND FUTURE PROSPECTS OF LANDBRIDGE SERVICES

AFTA enhancement of trade

Significant economic and social changes have taken place in ASEAN subregion. These changes include greater liberalization of economies and deregulation of services providing new challenges and opportunities for the countries in the region. The countries in the ASEAN subregion will continue with their efforts to improve their economic performance in the years to come. In this regard, regional cooperation will continue to be an important factor for improvement in transport efficiency.

Within ASEAN, the move towards AFTA will result in increase efforts to improve efficiency as well as increase economic integration among the members (allowing free trade and movements of resources among the member's countries). With a population of over 400 million, ASEAN will be an attractive market for product such as food, textile, footwear, consumer electronics and machineries and selected transport equipment. With the introduction of AFTA, business in the region will be forced to focus their efforts to rationalize their operations and improve their efficiency in order to face the increase in competition.

Cross border facilitation

ASEAN transport officials are organizing intergovernmental meetings to formulate policy and plan for free flow of goods and to enhance seamless movement of goods between countries in the ASEAN subregion.

Trans-Asian Railway Network in ASEAN subregion

Activities to develop the Trans-Asian Railway Network in the ASEAN subregion have mostly been carried out within the framework of the Singapore-Kunming Rail Link (SKRL) project pursued by the ASEAN secretariat since 1995. Under the project, the governments and railway organizations of the countries concerned have discussed the construction of the missing links to complete the three route options between the two cities. Related feasibility studies have been carried out either by the countries themselves or through the technical assistance of donor countries/agencies such as the Korea International Cooperation Agency for the missing link between Myanmar and Thailand, or China for the Cambodian section of the missing link between Cambodia and Viet Nam.

Completion of the missing link will allow rail to play a part in the economic integration of ASEAN by extending the reach of the container landbridge currently operated between Malaysia and Thailand to a range of destinations in other countries such as Cambodia, the Lao People's Democratic Republic and Viet Nam.

Challenges faced by landbridge service

The landbridge service has experienced growth for five consecutive years from its start in 1999 to 2004 in terms of both container throughput and revenue earnings. The volume of freight is however, currently on a declining trend due to capacity constraints on Thailand side because of shortage of locomotives. The service operators were also facing competition from larger and faster vessels now plying between Malaysian and Thai ports and from increasing competition from road hauliers.

CONCLUSION

Currently there are 28 weekly services between Klang Container Terminal Port Klang to Bangkok to Klang Container Terminal Port Klang and Singapore to Bangkok to Singapore. KTMB is also discussing with several potential landbridge operators to introduce new services between Kuala Lumpur and Bangkok. At the same time there exists potential of services from Pasir Gudang to Bangkok via the east-coast line in Sg. Golok.

There is no doubt that the landbridge services will contribute to promote the concept of borderless economy among the ASEAN countries. With the coming of AFTA and the proposed Trans-Asian Railway, KTMB has positioned itself to be a key player in free movement of goods in the ASEAN region. The service is expected to expand in the future by providing transit services to neighbouring countries of Cambodia, the Lao People's Democratic Republic and Viet Nam. In order to gain from the new opportunity provided by the AFTA framework, KTMB has positioned itself to be a key player in carrying freight traffic in the ASEAN subregion.

The landbridge service is a testimony of KTMB's commitment towards the setting up of the Trans-Asian rail link, the proposed rail network that has the potential to strengthen and enhance trade between ASEAN countries and China and beyond. With this prospect in mind KTMB is currently implementing projects to increase the capacity of the railway infrastructure in Malaysia, as well as making it suitable for the carriage of high containers, large refrigerated containers and dangerous goods.

Transport and Communications Bulletin for Asia and the Pacific

General guidelines for contributors

1. Manuscripts

One copy of the manuscript in English should be submitted together with a covering letter to the Editor indicating that the material has not been previously published or submitted for publication elsewhere. The author(s) should also submit a copy of the manuscript on computer diskette, labelled with the title of the article and the word-processing programme used, or by e-mail as an attachment file. MS Word and WordPerfect are the preferred word-processing programmes.

The length of the manuscript, including tables, figures and bibliographical references, may not exceed 7,500 words. Manuscripts should be typed on one side of A4 paper in double spacing and pages should be numbered. A list of references should be included. Manuscripts are subject to editorial revision.

The title page should contain: (a) title; (b) name(s) of the author(s); (c) institutional affiliation(s); (d) complete mailing address, e-mail address and facsimile number of the author, or of the principal author in the case of joint authors; and (e) an abstract of approximately 150 words clearly stating the main conclusions of the article. Acknowledgements, if any, should appear at the end of the text.

Articles should include a final section containing the main conclusions, which should be broadly intelligible to a non-specialist reader.

2. Tables

All tables should be clearly headed and numbered consecutively in Arabic numerals. They should be self-explanatory. All tables should be referred to in the text. Full source notes should be given below each table, followed by general notes, if any. Authors are fully responsible for the accuracy of the data.

3. Figures

All figures should be provided as camera-ready copy and numbered consecutively in Arabic numerals. All figures should be referred to in the text. Full source notes should be given below each figure.

4. Footnotes

Footnotes, if any, should be brief and numbered consecutively in superscript Arabic numerals. Footnotes should not be used for citing references.

5. References

There should be a complete reference for every citation in the text. References in the text should follow the author-date format, for example (Sadorsky, 1994), or (Skeldon, 1997: 243). Only those references actually cited in the text should be listed and these should appear in alphabetical order at the end of the manuscript. References should be in the following style:

[Book]
Skeldon, R. (1997). *Migration and Development: A Global Perspective* (London, Longman).

[Chapter in book]
Krueger, Alan, B. and Lawrence H. Summers (1987). Reflections on the inter-industry wage structure, in K. Lang and J.S. Leonard, eds., *Unemployment and the Structure of Labour Markets* (London, Blackwell), pp. 40-49.

[Article in journal]
Wachs, M. (1990). "Regulating traffic by controlling land use: the southern California experience", *Transportation,* vol. 16, No. 3, pp. 241-256.